THE LIFE OF
BLESSED
LOUISE DE MARILLAC

THE LIFE OF
BLESSED
LOUISE DE MARILLAC

CO-FOUNDRESS OF THE SISTERS OF
CHARITY OF SAINT VINCENT DE PAUL

Translated from the French of

PRINCE EMMANUEL DE BROGLIE

by

REV. JOSEPH LEONARD, C.M.

Caritas Christi urget nos

LONDON
BURNS OATES & WASHBOURNE LTD.
PUBLISHERS TO THE HOLY SEE

NIHIL OBSTAT:

EDUARDUS J. MAHONEY, S.TH.D.,
Censor deputatus.

IMPRIMATUR:

✠ JOSEPHUS BUTT,
Vicarius generalis.

WESTMONASTERII,
die 10a *Julii,* 1933.

Made and Printed in Great Britain
1933

INTRODUCTION

TO relate the life-story of the first Sister of Charity, to make known her work and the spirit that animated it is no easy matter;—far from it. By its very simplicity as much as by its greatness, and it may also be said by its incomprehensible fruitfulness, such an existence escapes, so to say, analysis and narration, as does everything that really comes from God. How indeed is one to tell the story worthily, truthfully, and unemphatically of what seems to have happened so naturally and at the same time so far beyond mere human understanding?

Everything is so simple in the life of Louise de Marillac, or Mademoiselle Le Gras, as, in accordance with the custom of the age, she was called after her marriage. Nothing brilliant, nothing apparently striking, nothing that attracts one's attention, is to be found there. Everything is unpretentious, commonplace even, at first sight, both in the work and the person of a woman who always strove to hide herself, and who feared above all to attract attention. And yet what we have to relate is the story of the foundress of one of the greatest works of Christian charity, the truest and most incontestably Christian, the most efficacious against suffering and evil, as well as for good, that this poor world has ever been given to contemplate. At the same time, the woman who has done this is likewise one of the purest and holiest souls that men can admire, one of those sublimely simple souls in which, without any extraordinary manifestation, the grace of God is reflected as in a mirror. Whether we like it or not, whether we have the faith or are unfortunately without it, when we have come to know such a soul and such a life, such pure and lofty virtue, such works accomplished with so much modesty and humility, destined as they were to produce such a harvest of succour and support for the poor and the humble of this world, we are compelled to admit that the finger of God is there, and that we are standing before one of His works.

Hence, without wishing to explain everything, or even striving to understand everything, we shall confine ourselves to a simple recital of the facts which will speak better and more loudly than anything we can say. Without going into minute details which might lead us far beyond the bounds of such a limited study as this, we shall strive to bring out the principal features that go to make up the essential originality of the figure we shall now endeavour to restore to life, if only for a moment ;— her perfect simplicity united with her unwearying activity, the ardour of her love for Jesus Christ revealing itself in an inexhaustible and untiring charity for his suffering members, the poor and the wretched. Those who would wish to know more of her and study the psychology of a saint, may, however, easily satisfy their desire in the pages of recent works in which scholarship and talent, charm and accuracy of knowledge, are conspicuous. In thus relating the life of Mademoiselle Le Gras briefly, dryly indeed at times, without any literary pretentions or even apologetic or controversial aim, our sole object is to reveal to those who may read these pages how the works decreed by God are accomplished, how those institutions He makes use of come into being, and the wide extent of good which, without noise or excited activity, may be realised here below by those who give themselves constantly and wholeheartedly to the fulfilment of His holy will.

The conclusion that naturally results from the spectacle we are now about to see unrolling before our eyes will be drawn solely from what is revealed, and words would but enfeeble it. In the presence of the first Sister of Charity at the head of the innumerable army of her daughters, and leading them, so to say, to the assault against suffering and evil in all its forms, silent admiration alone is fitting, and perhaps alone tolerable by her actual heirs and rivals. At the present moment, alas, they are scattered over all the roads of Europe and of the world, far from this land of France that saw their birth and does not know how to retain them ; but the sad times we are experiencing we confidently hope will soon pass.

CONTENTS

THE LIFE OF BLESSED
LOUISE DE MARILLAC

CHAPTER I

CHILDHOOD—MARRIAGE—WIDOWHOOD
1591–1628

LOUISE DE MARILLAC was born in Paris on August 12, 1591. She was the daughter of Louis de Marillac, Lord of the Manor of Ferrières, Councillor to the Parliament, and Margaret Le Camus, his second wife. The Marillacs were an old and sturdy race, long ennobled, deeply attached to the Bourbons and prominent for many years in public life. Under Louis XIII, two of Louis de Marillac's younger brothers were to become famous both by their brilliant fortune and tragic fall; Michel, Chancellor of France, and John, Marshal de Marillac, both victims of Richelieu's implacable policy. If Louise de Marillac was born into a family that took its place in the highest rank in society, she also came into a world—we shall not say in the crisis of revolution, for that phrase was not as yet invented and would not have been understood—but let us say in the midst of all the disturbances of the League and during Henry IV's siege of Paris. We know the horrors of those days which, let us hope, may never be revived.

Louise's mother, then, died shortly after the birth of her child, who came into the world weak and sickly, but, as every page of this story will show, with one of those finely tempered souls that triumph over every difficulty. ' God let me know,' she wrote long afterwards, ' that it was His will that I should go to Him by the Cross. From my birth and all through my life He has never left me without some occasion of suffering.' We shall see later how the child who thus entered upon life with a frail constitution and in the midst of political disturbances, learned how to walk in the way marked out for her. Very little indeed is known of her early years. Her father married again, for the third time, in 1595. His wife was Antoinette Camus, widow of the Lord of the Manor of Bréau, who had already three children of her own, two boys and a girl. As was then the custom, Louise was sent, when quite a young child, as a pupil to a convent. The celebrated monastery of Poissy was selected, and she was educated there under the guidance of Dominican nuns, of whom a certain Lady de Gondi was prioress. The education given in this famous convent replete with historical associations, was far from being as superficial or narrow as some moderns too easily believe about the education of young girls in those days. Far from it ;—it was an excellent and very wide education for the time. The young girls were taught

Latin and sometimes Greek, as well as the usual accomplishments of the period. Little Louise de Marillac had an aunt there who bore the same name as herself, who versified the office of the Blessed Virgin and the Penitential Psalms and wrote a paraphrase of the Canticle of Canticles, as well as other devotional works. She was therefore at a good school, but her father, perhaps, considered the education given there rather unsuitable for a child of modest fortune and too much designed for rich and illustrious young ladies destined to occupy a prominent place in society ; he withdrew her from Poissy and ' placed her in the hands of a skilful and virtuous schoolmistress to be taught how to perform the duties suitable to her rank in life.'

It was an abrupt change of surroundings to pass thus from the ranks of the highest nobility to those of the middle class and even the lower middle class, if we are to believe her biographers, for ' the good devout woman ' with whom she now stayed was poor. Louise learned from her not only how to manage a household but how to carry out all domestic tasks, even the roughest, and also various kinds of needlework. She did so without ever dreaming that it was an apprenticeship which would be most useful to her later, and would help in the fulfilment of God's designs in her regard. Moreover, her father, far from neglecting her, continued to watch over her carefully ; he put her through a course of sound and solid reading and even went as far as to have her ' taught philosophy to form her mind and enable her to proceed to still more elevated sciences.' Again, as he saw she had a disposition for painting, he had it carefully cultivated so that she learnt to draw and to paint. A few devotional miniatures and water-colour drawings, and even a large canvas, are still in existence, and reveal, we are told, a delicate taste and ' sound craftsmanship.' It need scarcely be said that religion and its exercises were not neglected in this education, and that even from her childhood, the daughter of this Councillor of the Parliament was carefully instructed in all Christian truths and received a sincere and solid training in piety.

As the soul of Louise de Marillac was naturally devout and fervent, it received this divine seed without any difficulty. The seed quickly took profound root so that from the very beginning she felt the urgent desire to lead a perfect Christian life. This was indeed a great moment in the religious life of France, one of those periods of renewal in which the Church, buffeted by tempests, seems called on to heal her wounds and to throw out fresh branches more living and fruitful than ever. On all sides the old religious orders were reorganising and at need reforming themselves, and new orders were coming into existence. Cardinal de Bérulle, with the help of Michel de Marillac, was bringing the Carmelite Order of S. Teresa and its austerities into France, whilst the astonished Parisians were moved at the sight of a procession of Capuchin nuns, barefooted and crowned with thorns, moving into their new convent in the Rue Saint-Honoré. Louise, moved at the sight of their austere life and strongly imbued with a penitential spirit, made up her mind to go and share their vocation. But as she was weak in body and frequently ill, her strength did not permit of her following out this generous inspiration. A Capuchin Father renowned for his virtues helped her to realise this and pointed out to her that the solemn promise which he believed she had made, formulated as it had been in a moment of exaltation, was not binding, and, in fact, was ' null and void.'

We mention this incident to show, as early as possible, the interior ardour of this soul which God was to call to such a lofty mission, and how, from the very first, she was filled with His love and a desire to manifest it.

Her father died about 1604, or some years later, but the date and circumstances of his death by which she was left an orphan are not known with certainty. She was thus deprived of a parent's love which seems to have been deep and true and to which she had responded with true daughterly tenderness. We may accept M. de Marillac's own testimony ; he said in his will that his daughter ' had been his greatest consolation in life, and had been given to him by God to soothe and calm his spirit.' The young girl, who was then about fifteen years old, thus found herself all alone and without the help and assistance of her parents. It was, however, at this period that the favour and influence of the Marillac family at Court was at its highest. One of Louise's uncles had married a niece of Marie de Medici, and the Queen's Superintendent of Finance, the Marquis d'Attichy, had become her uncle by his marriage with Valence de Marillac, her father's sister. Two other uncles were at the beginning of brilliant careers that were to end in disaster. She occupied therefore an excellent position in society, and it would seem as if she should have been much sought after in marriage. However, perhaps on account of her lack of wealth, it was only when she was twenty-two years of age, which was looked on as rather old in those days when life began much earlier and passed more rapidly than now, that Louise de Marillac married Anthony Le Gras. He came from an ancient family in Auvergne, was one of Marie de Medici's secretaries, and thus seemed destined for great things ; he was, moreover, ' a man of excellent life who greatly feared God and was most careful to keep himself beyond reproach.' The marriage took place in Paris on February 6, 1613, in the Church of Saint Gervais, and the young couple set up house in the parish of Saint Merry. It was there, at the end of that same year 1613, that Michel Le Gras, son of ' Mademoiselle Le Gras ' as she was called in accordance with the custom of the age, was born. He was a son to whom, according to S. Vincent de Paul, she was more than a mother, as our narrative will show.

Later on, they moved to the parish of Saint Saviour, ' Rue Courteau Villain ' (Cours au vilain), and set up house there in a style in harmony with their personal tastes and even with a certain amount of display, such as was demanded of persons of their rank by the ideas prevailing then. It was here that Mademoiselle Le Gras lived for some years, quite simply and uprightly, carrying out the duties imposed on her by her position in society ; nevertheless, from the first, and in the midst of the thousand temptations to which the brilliant prospects of her husband and family exposed her, she gave proof of her piety and of an active and intelligent charity towards the poor ; an example such as hers was then as now very rare, and at once put her in a place apart.[1]

'At that time,' an eye-witness tells us with touching simplicity, 'she showed great piety and devotion in serving the poor. She used to bring them dainties and sweet-meats, biscuits and other nice things. She combed their hair, cleansed them from scurf and vermin, and buried them when they died. She used to leave her visitors in order to climb a mountain and look after a poor man who shivered with the cold when it rained and hailed.' This picture makes us think even now of a Sister of Charity carrying out her duties towards the poor and miserable. It should be said that Mademoiselle Le Gras met with support and valuable advice from some of those around her ; they helped to make her a great Christian woman and to prepare her for the task to which God had destined her by thus training her to lead an inner life of the spirit, before confronting an active life and its dangers. Moreover, she was not exempt from those messengers of God, great trials. Her uncle, Michel de Marillac, Chancellor of France, who had translated the *Imitation of Christ* into French, and who spent as many hours in prayer in the Chapel of the Carmelite Nuns as he could snatch from the fulfilment of the duties of his office, carefully guided her in those first hours of fervour. The letters in which he tempers her zeal and uneasiness, whilst ever urging her on in the way

B

of perfection and renunciation, are fully worthy of
that great soul, who knew so well how to bear the
trial of the favour of the Court without being
dazzled by it for a moment, and then to lose it
without uttering a word of complaint or regret.
Mademoiselle Le Gras, thus instructed and prepared,
was now able to hear and comprehend the lessons
of a still greater master, Saint Francis de Sales,
whom she had the good fortune to meet in Paris,
moving in the very society in which she lived. She
was thus able to profit by the advice and direction
given her by word of mouth and intended for herself personally by one who knew so well how to
deal with individuals and whose mere presence was
the most valuable of all sermons.

In 1619, the Bishop of Geneva and the Cardinal
of Savoy spent six months in Paris engaged in
diplomatic negotiations. As he was in close touch
with Michel de Marillac, whom he had met during
former visits to Paris, Mademoiselle Le Gras was
fortunate enough to be able to enjoy his society
and also to hear the discourses of a Saint who was
then, as now, regarded as one of the greatest masters
of the spiritual life. She never forgot the lessons
of him whom she loved to call ' her blessed Father.'
No doubt it was to him she owed that amiable and
gracious type of devotion which is one of the
characteristic marks of all those who had drunk
even a little from this source. When the Bishop of
Geneva, towards the end of 1619, left Paris, to
which he was never to return, he handed her over
to the care of the Bishop of Belley, John Camus, his
chosen disciple, whose great reputation as a preacher

caused him to be invited every year to Paris. He, like his master, was a great spiritual guide : he was not slow to see that Mademoiselle Le Gras was a ' clear and strong-minded ' woman who still had, however, ' some weaknesses and failings.'

His direction came at a very suitable moment, because Mademoiselle Le Gras was just then suffering from some of those interior trials that are never spared to souls whom God wishes to make use of for the fulfilment of his designs. They might almost be called the novitiate of the interior life which alone renders one apt for the works of the active life.

At the end of 1622, her husband fell ill of a disease that soon proved to be incurable. Louise, who nursed him with devotion and care, was so disturbed by this unexpected blow that she looked upon it as a punishment for her infidelity to her former promise, and believed that she was the cause of her husband's illness. Her distress of mind was so intense that she made a vow never to re-marry, if she should have the misfortune to lose her husband, and to devote herself entirely to the service of God. She made this promise to which she was to adhere so loyally, on May 24, 1623, the feast of S. Monica. She felt at first some mental relief but quickly relapsed into ' a profound state of depression.' She asked herself whether she was not bound to leave her husband in order to carry out what she called her first vow so as to be at greater liberty to serve God and her neighbour, and if she should not change her spiritual guide ; finally, she was assailed by doubts on the immortality of the soul, and these doubts, as she tells us in a note written in her own hand, were prompting her ' not to believe in the Divinity.' For several days this poor soul, whom we shall see later so strong and brave, was a prey to the most bitter anguish of mind, but she bore it with the humility and submission which always succeed in securing deliverance. On the feast of Pentecost, 1623, as she tells us,[2] ' whilst I was at Mass in the Church of S. Nicholas in the Fields, my mind was completely cleared of these doubts, and I was told that I should remain with my husband, and that a time would come when I should be able to make vows of poverty, chastity and obedience, and that this would be in the company of others, some of whom would do the same. I then understood that I should be in a place where I could serve my neighbour but I could not understand how this could come about, because there was to be much coming and going.

' I was also told that I should remain tranquil, as far as my director was concerned, and that God would give me one whom, as I think, he then let me see, and I felt a repugnance to accept him. Nevertheless, I acquiesced, and it seemed to be my duty not to make any change just then. My third anxiety was removed by the certainty I experienced in my mind that it was God who was teaching me what I have just said, and that as it was God, I should have no further doubt. At this period, doubts about immortality were inclining me not to believe in the Divinity. I have always believed I received this grace through the blessed Bishop of Geneva, as before his death I had greatly desired to tell him about these temptations and ever since have had a great devotion to him, and I have by his means received many graces ; and at this time I had a certain reason to believe it, which I no longer recollect.'

These lines furnish a sort of prophetic résumé of the life and work of Mademoiselle Le Gras, and are so striking that they deserve to be quoted in full, even in this short history. The persons with whom she was to live, observing the vows of poverty, chastity, and obedience, in order to help their neighbour, was the Company of the Daughters of Charity, who ' came and went,' that is to say, who lived outside the cloister in a manner she could not then understand. The director whom she received from God's hand, without nature having the least part in it, was doubtless ' M. Vincent,' and the unwavering, simple, naked faith, that of the Sister of Charity who leads back to God the sick whose wounds she tends.

At the end of this same year 1623, the Bishop of Belley, who was expected in Paris to preach a course of Advent sermons, could not come, to the great disappointment of Mademoiselle Le Gras who had been counting on his arrival. Her disappointment was all the greater seeing that her husband, who was growing more and more ailing, seemed likely to be carried off in the next paroxysm of his illness, and everything indicated that his death was close at hand. The Bishop of Belley wrote letters to her intended for her consolation and to induce her to accept ' the most loving Will of God who renders all things amiable.' Poor Mademoiselle Le Gras was, in fact,

fully occupied with nursing her husband, whose
character was embittered by suffering and who fell
into fits of profound melancholy. She was unconsciously going through her apprenticeship as a
Sister of Charity, and it would seem as if Mgr
Camus had a presentiment of this when he wrote
her the following lines : ' Mademoiselle, my dear
daughter, I sympathise with your anxiety of mind
about the illness of your husband. Well now, that
is your cross, and how can I be disturbed at seeing
it laid on the shoulders of a daughter of the Cross ?
You are not lacking in skill, in advice, in books or
in knowledge of how to bear it well. May God
also grant you may not be lacking in courage.'[3]

The year 1624 was to prove decisive in the life of
Mademoiselle Le Gras and destined to supply the
help and guidance needed to stimulate the ardour
of her love for God and his poor, and to render it,
as the event proved, fruitful. It was the year in
fact in which she began to be guided by S. Vincent
de Paul, or ' M. Vincent ' as he was then called, and
in which he finally consented to act as her spiritual
director. The first meeting of those two, so well
fitted to understand each other, which was to have
such great consequences for the good of souls by
relieving the wants and sufferings of the poor and
sick, was no doubt perfectly simple, and occurred
without anyone taking the slightest notice of it.
So we must omit any oratorical or literary comment
to which such a meeting might lend itself and say
once for all that it was in the course of 1624 that
M. Vincent, who was still tutor to the De Gondi
children, agreed, though not without some reluct-

ance, to undertake the spiritual direction of S. Louise de Marillac. Since the Bishop of Belley's departure, she had felt rather abandoned and was looking about for a guide. She must frequently have seen M. Vincent in her parish church of S. Saviour's, which was also that of the De Gondis who were living in the Rue Pavée, and where M. Vincent often went to say Mass. We do not know if the rather cold and dry manner, which the saint himself tells us he found hard to shake off, had made Louise hold aloof from him and experience the repugnance to which she alludes above. But the fact remains that until then they had not ' conferred,' to use the phrase then current, and this only came about when, doubtless at the Bishop of Belley's request, M. Vincent consented to take over the spiritual direction of Mademoiselle Le Gras. But these two souls were too much alike in their love of God and of their neighbour to waste much time before understanding each other : an *entente* was very soon reached. With his admirable ' discernment of spirit ' which was conjoined in perfect harmony with his inexhaustible charity, S. Vincent quickly detected the hidden treasures of zeal, ardour, and profound and active love of others in this apparently weak and sickly young woman, who was so easily perturbed and who seemed so unlikely to perform heroic deeds. As for Mademoiselle Le Gras, she no sooner had heard S. Vincent's words of advice and replies to her questions than she realised that this was the director of whom she had been told, and she opened out her heart and soul to him as to one who was to be henceforth her support, adviser, and guide in the ways that lead to God. This is clear from the following brief remarks sent to her by Mgr Camus, the Bishop of Belley, during a brief absence of her director: 'Forgive me, my dearest sister,' he wrote on July 26, 1624, that is to say, a few months after S. Vincent's first interview with Mademoiselle Le Gras, 'forgive me for saying that you attach yourself a little too much to those who direct you, and rely on them a little too much. Here is M. Vincent in eclipse, and Mademoiselle Le Gras quite upset and disconcerted. We should see God in our directors and our directors in God. But at times we should regard only God, who, without men or a Pool of Probatica, can cure us of our paralysis. . . . Not, dear soul, that it is any trouble to guide or advise you. No, quite the contrary, for I trust through this guidance that you will guide me to Heaven, to which your example invites me much more than my advice helps you on the journey thither. But I do not care to see in Mademoiselle Le Gras' mind, which I esteem so highly and which seems to me to be both clear and strong, those little clouds and weaknesses.'[4] Mademoiselle Le Gras was soon to be in need of all that strength of mind to which the bishop appealed, for her husband's condition was growing worse and the end was approaching. S. Vincent was just then in Provence, and Louise was left all alone to face those trying hours.

Towards the end of December 1625, after an attack of brain fever, which had almost carried him off six weeks previously, Anthony Le Gras breathed his last sigh in the arms of his wife who, alone with

he should be loved, for he has deprived you of what you loved so dearly. . . . Now is the time for one to ask God to remember his word ; and what, my dearest daughter, is that word ? It is that he will be a father to the orphan and a judge to the widow, a judge, my dear sister, who will take her cause in hand and judge her adversaries. . . .'[6]

In 1626, Louise de Marillac, widow of Anthony Le Gras, secretary to Queen Marie de Medicis, celebrated her thirty-fifth birthday on August 12. She had spent thirteen years in the bonds of wedlock, living in the midst of the world to which she had quietly given an example of all the domestic virtues, and yet had never ceased from labouring with undiminished zeal and ardour at her interior perfection and progress in devotion.

The hour had now sounded for her to cultivate the field of the Householder, to employ the phraseology of those days, and to return, laden with the sheaves of a rich harvest. The moment had indeed come, without her ever dreaming of it, when the modest widow, who shunned rather than desired to attract attention, was to put her hand to a work destined to produce incalculable good to the Church and to bring inestimable help to all the poor and afflicted. Children, the poor and the sick, were to find in the work to which Louise de Marillac now devoted her attention—their schools, their humble dwellings, and their hospitals—not only attention to all their material needs but also the spiritual instruction they required. She taught them these lessons with an inexhaustible and loving devotion, and always accompanied her material

ministrations with the Christian consolations of the
teachings of religion, the place of which can never
be taken by all the remedies or the science of this
world.   Louise de Marillac (as we shall continue
to call her, and sometimes Mademoiselle Le Gras,
in accordance with the custom of the time) would
have been more surprised than anyone if such a
destiny had been foretold her ; she would, doubtless, have completely put aside the idea of serving
as an instrument of Providence for such a work.
But the ways of God, though often mysterious and
seemingly shrouded in mists, are none the less His
ways and always attain their ends.   The narrative
of the life of Mademoiselle Le Gras henceforward
will furnish us with another example of this truth.
She laboured, at first, and almost without perceiving
it, at the foundation of the Sisters of Charity, under
the guidance of S. Vincent de Paul.   Once the work
had been created and received recognition, the
foundress, who never resisted even in the slightest
the manifest will of ' the good God,' continued
incessantly to watch over its beginnings.   She never
abandoned her task until death came to tell her it
was now time to rest in God, and she did it all
simply, quietly, noiselessly, as if it were always the
simplest thing in the world : a true sister of charity
before the event, if I may use the phrase.   This is
what we are now about to show briefly by giving
an account of her relations with S. Vincent de Paul
and of all the good that thereby ensued.

The *Confraternities of Charity* which that great
man had just established, and which were multiplying with extraordinary rapidity, were the first to

profit by the good will of Mademoiselle Le Gras, and the great leisure now at her disposal. But above all else, it was essential to train the labourer before asking her to form and watch over others, and this she herself was the first to recognise and desire.

Hence, of her own accord, she left her house in the Marais which was, in the beginning of the seventeenth century, the rich and fashionable quarter, and went to live in an old, broken-down mansion, in the Rue Saint-Victor. But this street, situated on the hill of Saint Genevieve, was close to the Collège des Bons-Enfants which Madame de Gondi had just presented to Saint Vincent. The latter had taken up his residence there together with his missionaries and it was the cradle of his congregation, which is now called ' Lazarists '⁷ from the House of Saint-Lazare, an order of chivalry then in decay, which was granted to him somewhat later. There, quite close to S. Vincent, to whom she had committed the direction of her soul and the guidance of her life, and who was himself set at liberty by the death of Madame de Gondi in 1625 and had just begun to reside in the Bons-Enfants, she could work away peacefully and quietly at her own perfection. It was here she prepared herself in prayer and silence for a mission still unknown to her, but to which she had been destined by God. She made retreats, notes of which have been preserved, and read spiritual books as well as meditating on the truths of religion and reciting her vocal prayers. The rule of life she laid down for herself when she entered this new abode in which she meant to inaugurate a new life, has been preserved, and would be well worth giving in its entirety, did space permit. It reads almost like the actual rule of the Sisters of Charity, if one will just observe that it is primarily concerned with a person still living in the world who had duties to fulfil there, and who had fully determined to carry them out in their entirety.

Louise de Marillac intended to make two retreats every year, each lasting eight days, either in a community or simply in her own house, and the subject matter of her meditations was to be taken from those placed by the Bishop of Geneva at the beginning and end of his *Introduction to a Devout Life*.

' Write to me every second day,' S. Vincent told her, ' a summary of all that occurs and the dispositions of your mind and body ; strive above everything else not to be over-earnest but do all things peacefully, as you may imagine the dear Bishop of Geneva used to do. I forgot to tell you that you should not overburthen yourself with rules or pious practices, but should fortify yourself well to carry out carefully whatever ones you observe, your daily actions, your employments ; in short, let everything be directed towards doing well whatever you actually perform ; no longer entertain for a moment those peculiar ideas which formerly use to harass you ; this is only a trick the evil spirit wishes to play on you.' Mademoiselle Le Gras, at her director's request, drew up a résumé of her reflections during her retreats. Some of these have been preserved and they will help us, after all these years, to appreciate her spiritual state at the conclusion of these exercises in which she succeeded in training herself for the work for which God had reserved her. Here are one or two extracts which will enable us to hear her speaking for herself and which, moreover, are interesting inasmuch as they are written in that grave, simple style so characteristic of the age and bearing the marks of an inimitable originality. What she desires above all, as we may see from these remarks, is to bear the stamp of Jesus Christ by the imitation of his virtues.[8] 'I am bound,' she writes, 'willingly to render up to Jesus the possession of my soul, as he has rightly been made its King, and I will cherish the joy I experience on seeing this desire in myself, and his power to make each one of us in particular his well-beloved friend.'

'I desired no longer to subsist in myself, but having been continually sustained by God's graces, it seemed to me *that my whole being was nothing but graces.*' Hence she will gladly spend her days in following Him and in considering what Jesus would have done in every action of her life.[9] 'When passing before the Most Holy Sacrament, I felt inwardly but very strongly urged, and I will gladly place myself in a state of holy indifference *so as to be more disposed to accept God's call and to carry out his most holy will,* regarding myself as unworthy that his loving kindness should have any designs on my soul; and I desire that his designs be entirely fulfilled in me, and I wish to offer myself to God all my life for that end.'

During the retreats before Christmas, she frequently meditated on the Crib which she called

' the throne of the Kingdom of holy poverty.'[10]
' I ardently desired to be admitted to it,' she says,
' as this virtue of poverty is most loved by the King
of the Poor, and He makes this known by the fact
that whilst poverty is to be found all over the world,
He is only recognised by those who are poor in
simplicity and truth, and on that account, He made
known His birth by the voice of angels, so as to
make it certain that it is God Himself who honours
this state.'

' To participate in this grace, it is necessary, after
the example of the shepherds, to correspond without delay to His holy inspirations.' She desired ' to
imitate, in deed and not merely in desire, the Holy
Child of Bethlehem who, being rich, chose holy
poverty and obedience by which He made Himself
subject to the Blessed Virgin and S. Joseph.' ' I
beseech Him with all my heart to give me the grace
to imitate Him in this, even though I am so unworthy
of it, trusting to His divine goodness that, having
given me a desire to do so for so long a time, He
may bestow it upon me in reality.' This perfect
submission to the will of God, to which she aspired
so sincerely, even when she felt herself far removed
from it, led her to take resolutions such as the
following which clearly show that the work of
formation was being rapidly accomplished in her.
She resolved ' to hold herself hidden in God, without seeking the testimony of creatures, being content that God sees what she desires to be.' She
returns to this point again, in other places, with an
insistence that is surely significant : ' In imitation
of the Blessed Virgin, I am bound to give myself

to God to serve my neighbour in a condition subject to reproach in the eyes of the world, imitating our Lord, who all His life despised His temporal interest for the advantage of His creatures ; and this I desire to do if it be His holy will.' And again : ' I will accept the choice that Jesus wishes I should make of the lowliest manner in which I can serve Him,' and in a ' place least subject to the world's approval.'[11]

But this profound and sincere humility neither cooled nor diminished her zeal; she wished to work for God's glory, and believed, in spite of her delicate health and the slight amount of weight attaching to her position as a simple gentlewoman, that she could do so efficaciously, just because she expected everything from the grace of God and nothing from herself.

' The apostles,' she writes during a retreat made during the Octave of Pentecost, ' were not content with merely going to find Jesus on the mountain where he had promised to appear, but, by their word and example, they brought a great number of people thither, and this is what I should strive to imitate, as far as I can : procuring the salvation of my neighbour for the glory of God.'[12]

In this way, Mademoiselle Le Gras was preparing herself in solitude and prayer to labour with all her strength at the fulfilment of God's will, the nature and extent of which she was still in ignorance. If she was still unaware of the task which she was to accomplish, and this want of knowledge must have been for her one of the trials laid by God on those whom He has destined for great things, we shall

c

see in a moment that even if S. Vincent de Paul had to calm her mind on this point and induce her to be patient, she was none the less firmly resolved to give and consecrate herself entirely to God without any reserve or any going back.   It is she herself who tells us so in an act of consecration which she drew up during these years of preparation and recollection.   It has been preserved, and, despite its length, deserves to be reproduced here.   Even though she writes in the rather diffuse and involved style of the beginning of the seventeenth century, we may, nevertheless, easily detect the elevation and greatness of soul to which she had reached when she could find words so replete with sincerity and a true love of God.

' I, the undersigned,' she says, ' in the presence of the everlasting God, having considered that on the day of my baptism I was vowed and dedicated to my God to be His daughter, and that, nevertheless, I have repeatedly sinned against His most holy will ; also considering the immense mercy of the love and sweetness with which this most good God has ever maintained this desire in me, notwithstanding an almost continual resistance, of which I am most gravely culpable, and although I have all my life neglected and slighted the graces which His goodness has bestowed on me, and they have been very great in my regard, wretched and unworthy creature that I am ;

' And, finally, coming back to myself, I detest with all my heart the iniquities of my whole past life, which render me guilty of treason against God and of the death of Jesus Christ, and would merit that I should be damned more than Lucifer ; yet, trusting in the infinite mercifulness of my God, I ask Him with all my heart for forgiveness and plenary absolution both for the sins of which I have accused myself and for those I forget and especially for the way in which I abused the sacraments, which cannot have taken place without great contempt of His goodness, of which I now repent with all my heart, relying on the merits of my Saviour's death for my soul, as being the only grounds of my hope, in virtue of which I avow and renew the sacred profession made on my behalf to God at my baptism, and now irrevocably resolve to serve and to love Him with greater fidelity, giving myself wholly to Him.   And on this account, I also renew the vow I made of my widowhood and of my resolutions to practise the holy virtues of humility, obedience, poverty, and suffering in honour of the same virtues in Jesus Christ, which He has so often inspired in me by His love.

'I protest, furthermore, that I will never again offend God in any part of my being, and will abandon myself wholly to the design of His holy Providence for the accomplishment of His holy will in me, and I now dedicate and sacrifice myself to God's Providence for ever, and choose it for my sovereign consolation.

'But if, through my customary weakness, it should happen that I break these holy resolutions, which God in His goodness forbid, I now implore the help of the Holy Spirit, to grant me at once the grace of conversion, as I fervently desire never for a single moment to be displeasing to God.   This

is my irrevocable determination, which I confirm
in the presence of God and of the Blessed Virgin,
of my angel guardian and of all the saints, in the
sight of the Church militant which is listening to
me, in the presence of my spiritual Father who,
holding the place of God in my regard, can, if he
pleases, by his charitable guidance, assist me in the
execution of these resolutions and aid me to accomplish the most holy will of God by obedience to
him in this matter.

'O my God, mayst thou be pleased to strengthen
these holy resolutions and this consecration of
myself, and accept them as an odour of sweetness
since thou hast been pleased to inspire me with
them; give me the grace, O my God, to carry
them out perfectly; Thou art my God and my all,
and I now recognise and adore Thee as such, one,
only, true God in three Persons now and for ever-
more.   Live our love and that of Jesus crucified!

LOUISE DE MARILLAC.'

This act of consecration, which seems to have
been written in 1627, reveals to us, so to say, the
secret of Louise de Marillac's soul shortly after she
had become a widow and was thus once more free
and mistress of herself.   We may here see to what
extent she had given herself entirely to God from
the very beginning, and only aspired to serve Him
with all her soul and strength.   This is also evident
from the rule of life of which we have spoken and
which dates from the same period.   Far from having
to urge her on, S. Vincent had, on the contrary, to
restrain the zeal of his penitent, all on fire as she

was to labour for the glory of God and anxious to
devote herself immediately to some special work.
But her guide, with his usual wisdom and discretion, was anxious to lay the foundations of
Christian perfection on a solid basis, and made her
wait patiently and for a period which she at times
regarded as too protracted.   One day when he knew
she was ill, he wrote and asked her not to visit the
poor people whom she was then nursing as was
laid down in her rule of life :

' I request you,'[13] he wrote, ' not to go to the
poor to-day.   In this way you will honour the
inaction of the Son of God who will communicate
to you the grace of compassion for the sick, as well
as for the whole human race, by making you feel
your own powerlessness to accomplish what your
fervour desires.'   ' *Mon Dieu* my daughter,' he said
on another occasion, and he often repeated the
remark, ' what great treasures are hidden in Holy
Providence, and how those persons sovereignly
honour our Lord who follow and never anticipate
It ! " Oh yes ! " you may say to me, " but is it
not for God that I thus distress myself ? " If you
distress yourself in order to serve God, then it is no
longer for God you are labouring when you thus
distress yourself. . . .[14]   And as for what you are
to do, so far my heart has not been sufficiently
enlightened before God about a certain difficulty
which prevents me from seeing if it be really the
will of His divine Majesty. I beg you, Mademoiselle,
to recommend this matter to Him during those days
in which He pours forth the graces of the Holy
Ghost in greater abundance.'

Mademoiselle Le Gras, on her side, wrote down in her resolutions :[15] ' I will persevere in awaiting the coming of the Holy Ghost, although I am utterly ignorant of the time of His coming. But whilst accepting this state of ignorance and want of knowledge of the ways by which God intends me to serve Him, I will abandon myself entirely to Him, and prepare my soul ; I will voluntarily renounce all things to follow Him.'

The pupil, as we may see, was worthy from the very beginning of the master who thus exhorted her to patience and that total abandonment to God of which he himself gave the example. As a matter of fact, it was at this very time that he was busy establishing those ' Charities ' which were to lead up unconsciously to the foundation of the Sisters of Charity who were originally intended merely to assist this enterprise, a fact soon to be forgotten.

We cannot here enter into details of this attempt by S. Vincent de Paul to regulate, and thus render as useful as possible, almsgiving that was frequently ineffectual and abused, and to get the most out of it. This it was that gave rise to the ' Charities ' and through them to the Daughters of Charity. We shall relate only what is indispensable if we are to realise the part which was soon to be played in this matter by Louise de Marillac, and the manner in which, as unconsciously as her spiritual father, she became, without definitely planning or intending it, the co-foundress of one of the great Christian enterprises of modern times. She was at this time thinking solely of how to occupy herself usefully in aiding and comforting the poor, a form of activity which to her mind was somewhat neglected. Rarely has the action of divine grace, at first so hidden and insensible and then so strong and irresistible, been more clearly revealed or better outlined.

From 1617, S. Vincent had been endeavouring to establish charitable associations wherever he could ; he collected together ' a certain number of ladies or girls who were admitted only with the consent of their husbands or fathers and mothers and who called themselves *servants of the poor*.' They were all free, voluntary workers who endeavoured to regulate equitably, justly, and intelligently the administration of alms destined for the relief of the poor, so as to avoid waste and faulty distribution. ' The end for which this confraternity was set up,' wrote Mademoiselle Le Gras, in a note[16] intended for one of the earliest set of regulations of the first ' charities,' ' is to assist the sick poor of the parish : spiritually, by seeing that those who are dying may depart from this life in a good state, and that those who recover may be resolved nevermore to offend God. And corporally, by distributing to them whatever they may need in the way of food and medicines ; and finally, to accomplish our Lord's ardent desire that we should love one another.' The patron of the association ' shall be our Lord who is Charity itself.'[17] The members are to learn to know the poor by personal contact, visiting them and bringing with them food and medicine. They could also, whilst tending their bodies in their needs and maladies, pay attention to their souls, which are frequently in even greater need, by teaching

the living how to lead a good life, and the dying
how to die well, by bringing back individuals to
the practice of their religion, and by preparing a
way, in the case of the sick and dying, for the priest
who might otherwise be neither admitted or called
in.'

These 'charities' multiplied very rapidly in the
district round Paris. Mademoiselle Le Gras was
very soon employed by S. Vincent in this work,
whilst she was still living in her own home, and
carrying on her usual manner of life and ordinary
occupations. Whilst he was moving around the
suburbs of Paris, in his capacity of missionary,
establishing 'charities' and scattering the good
seed of the Word in all directions, caring for bodies
after instructing and purifying souls, Mademoiselle
Le Gras was sending him whatever alms she had
collected, and carrying out his commissions and
whatever works he confided to her care. On one
occasion, she sent him fifty *livres* which he had
asked for the confraternity of 'Verneuil in the
Beauvais district,' which was intended to combat
certain enterprises undertaken by the Huguenots
who were very active in that province. ' You will
do me the favour,' he wrote to her,[18] ' of assuring
the person who gave you the alms that our Lord
himself will recompense her well, and that I have
begun to apply your *livres*, as I am in this place,
to the setting-up of the Charity which is being
established here, where we have found much
temporal as well as spiritual destitution, as a number
of Huguenots who are here, take occasion of the
help they give the poor to corrupt them, thus doing

unspeakable harm. You might send us four more
shirts, and please present my most humble respects
to your kind young lady.' On another occasion,
S. Vincent requested Louise de Marillac to find
a house for some poor girls whom he wished to
remove from surroundings that were most unsuitable ; this alone goes to show the confidence he
already had in his retiring co-worker who so far
had not made any appearance. On January 18,
1628, he writes to her,[19] ' Prepare in the meantime
to perform an act of charity for two poor girls who
it seems to us should leave here, and who will call
on you eight days hence, and we beg you to send
them to some respectable woman who will find
a place for them, if you do not know of any lady
who is in need of them. We shall have work to do
here for about six weeks and after that I shall be
entirely at your disposal.' Some days later, he
thanks her for having taken one of these girls into
her own house, and also for different packages sent
to the ' charity ' with which he was then concerned.
In this way, S. Vincent de Paul, whilst training her
interiorly in Christian perfection, was also giving
her a practical preparation for the mission to which
she was destined by God. She practised charity
and loved and cared for the poor, before teaching
others to do so ; she fashioned herself in silence and
prayer before labouring at the formation of others.

But the works of God, which begin as a rule in
silence and obscurity, are none the less destined to
develop and fructify abundantly ; a day arrives
when they come out into the sunshine and reveal
themselves in all their beauty and efficaciousness.

The moment was not far off when Louise de Marillac was to take up the work that God intended her to carry out, but it was essential that she should first be able to say to herself that she had discharged to the full the obligations which she still owed to society, and fulfilled them in their entirety. In 1628, Michel Le Gras, whom she looked after with a true mother's love and care, became a pupil in the seminary of S. Nicholas du Chardonnet. This was a house for young clerics who intended to be priests and had been founded by Adrian Bourdoise, one of the most learned priests of the time. Louise de Marillac's son was at this time fourteen years old and weak both in character and constitution; he seemed to have some inclination for the priesthood and was sent to Bourdoise to be tested, and if he had a vocation, to afford it an opportunity to ripen. Mademoiselle Le Gras busied herself with her son's education with such passionate care and tenderness that S. Vincent saw himself at times forced to restrain her:[20] 'If you are a woman of courage,' he wrote to her one day, 'you will lay aside your little triflings and motherly softnesses. I have never seen a mother who was so much of a mother as you. You are not like a woman in any other respect.'

Michel's entrance into the seminary of S. Nicholas du Chardonnet, where we may as well at once say he remained only for a few years and which he left without taking orders, broke the last link that bound Louise de Marillac to the world and the society of her time. She was free to devote herself completely to the works for which she had been training herself ever since the death of her husband. The Master was about to call her to Himself, and His call would find her ready, her lamp alight, her heart detached and her hands fashioned for hard tasks. Henceforward, she was no longer to be a Christian woman living in the world, but a Sister of Charity, leading the life of the cloister in the world, and inaugurating a new form of the religious life, fruitful in most unexpected results, which we shall now see unfolding before our eyes. Yet again we should admire in silence the inimitable ways of Providence which creates so many and such great things with so little noise or commotion and by means so apparently out of proportion to their effects.

NOTES ON CHAPTER I

[1] *Louise de Marillac*, par Mgr Baunard, Paris. Poussielgue, 1898, p. 14.

[2] *Louise de Marillac, Sa vie, Ses vertus, Son esprit*, Vol. II, p. 128.

[3] Baunard, *op. cit.*, p. 28.

[4] Baunard, *op. cit.*, p. 32.

[5] *La vie de Mademoiselle Le Gras, fondatrice et première supérieure de la Compagnie des Filles de la Charité*, par l'Abbé Gobillon, Paris. A. Pralard, 1676, p. 18.

[6] Baunard, *op. cit.*, p. 36.

[7] The Priests of the Congregation of the Mission (Lazarists) are known in English-speaking countries as ' Vincentians.'

[8] Louise de Marillac, *Écrits et Pensées*, p. 31.

[9] *Ibid.*, p. 14.

[10] *Ibid.*, p. 28.

[11] *Ibid.*, p. 29.

[12] *Ibid.*, p. 7.

CHAPTER II

THE ' charities ' first established by S. Vincent de Paul in the provinces about the year 1617, had multiplied and developed with a surprising rapidity in the districts round Paris, Saint-Cloud, Suresnes, and still farther away at Beauvais and the surrounding country, and at Montmirail on the De Gondi estates. The head of that family had by this time become a priest and entered the Congregation of the Oratory. In 1623, S. Vincent preached missions in Burgundy and established ' charities ' at Bourg, Mâcon and Chalon-sur-Saône, but so far no branch had yet been established in Paris. It was not indeed enough to erect confraternities such as these which had from the first shown their utility and developed so rapidly ; it was also essential to supervise them, to maintain good order and to see that they were carrying out properly the work for which they had been instituted. Now to do this, since each ' charity ' remained independent, there was need of a common purpose and a general supervision. S. Vincent, overburdened as he was with preaching sermons and giving missions and with the establishment and direction of his new

Congregation, could not possibly attempt this work; and indeed it was one better fitted for a woman, for it had from the beginning been confided to women, and they were carrying it out with energy and zeal.

Now, it was just at this moment that Mademoiselle Le Gras, who was more than ever afflicted by the idea, as she believed, of her own uselessness, found herself free from every tie and obligation. Her son, who was never absent from her mind and thoughts, was, as we have just said, a boarder in Bourdoise's seminary, and her widowhood had quietly and as it were naturally set her apart from the world and even from her own family which was then at the height of its worldly success before being plunged into the depths of disgrace. She was therefore marked out in a special way to play the part of which we have spoken. S. Vincent de Paul, who knew her thoroughly and was well aware that no one could play this part more efficiently, made no delay in asking her to take it up. Louise de Marillac, on her side, did not hesitate for a moment before accepting it. It does not seem likely that either the one or the other or both had any secret presentiment of the greatness of the work which was to be the result of this first and difficult mission of Mademoiselle Le Gras, for there is no indication whatever of such an expectation; if it existed, it has remained hidden in God.

In the month of May 1629, S. Vincent requested Louise de Marillac to make a visitation in his name of the 'charities' in the provinces. Accordingly she set out on May 6, 1629, and the date has ever remained dear to all her innumerable daughters because it marks the beginning, the definite entry of their mother into that active religious life which she was to extend so widely by giving it a new form, more in accordance with the needs of the age, and which nothing so far could lead the public to anticipate.

On the day of her departure, S. Vincent wrote to her: ' So set out then, Mademoiselle, in the name of our Lord. I beseech His divine Goodness to accompany you, and may It be your solace by the way, your protection against the heat of the sun, your shelter against rain and cold, your soft bed in weariness and languor, your strength in your labours, and may It finally bring you back to us in perfect health, laden with good works.

' You might go to Holy Communion on the day you set out, in honour of the charity of our Lord and the journeys He made for that same end and out of the same charity, and of the pains, contradictions, weariness and labours He underwent, and that He may be pleased to bless your journey, to grant you His spirit and the grace to act in that same spirit and to bear your troubles in the manner in which He bore His. . . . I think it will be enough if you remain for one or two days in each place on your first visit, for you could return there next summer in case our Lord lets it be seen that you may be able to render Him some further service. When I say two days, you will remain longer in case there be any necessity, and you will do us the kindness of writing to us. . . . Adieu, Mademoiselle, remember us in your prayers, and, above all else, take care of your health, which I pray

God to preserve. . . .'[1]   On the morning of her
departure Louise went to Holy Communion in
accordance with her director's advice, and then,
furnished with letters of introduction and instructions as to what she was to do on her journey, both
of which had been prepared for her by S. Vincent,
she took the Champagne coach for Montmirail.
But the coach, which was in those days a rapid and
excellent form of transport, did not bring her to the
end of her first ' apostolic' journey.   To reach the
outlying villages she had to face bad roads, uncom-
fortable carts, dirty lodging-houses, and at times she
had to go by wagon or even on horse-back.   She
cheerfully welcomed all such difficulties ' so as to
have a greater share in the miseries of the poor.'
Unfortunately, we have no details about her first
journey ; we only know from her first biographer
that she visited with the greatest care the confraternities established in Montmirail and its
environs, all of which were on the De Gondi
estates, brought with her or procured for the poor
the attention and care of which they were in need,
without omitting to supply, when she was able,
' those various little comforts ' which are sometimes
so useful in these circumstances.   In this way she
inaugurated a tradition which has been faithfully
followed by her daughters.   She also inspected, if
the word be not too official, the manner in which
the ladies or the peasant women who were members
of the confraternity and who were even then called
' the servants of the poor,' carried out their self-
imposed tasks.   She let them have the results of
her own experience so as to enable them to procure

the greatest possible fruit from their good will and good works, both for the bodies and souls of their poor protégés. At the end of the summer she returned to Paris and submitted to S. Vincent the remarks and observations he had asked for. The result of Louise de Marillac's tour, far from discouraging S. Vincent in his enterprise, only served to increase his zeal and ardour. Indeed it was in that same autumn of 1629 that the first 'charities' were established in Paris, and these were destined to furnish him with an opportunity of definitely founding a new religious family.

As a matter of fact, he had for some time desired to establish the work in Paris and had even made an attempt ' at the request of the Procurator-General,' but it had proved unsuccessful. This time, aided by Mademoiselle Le Gras, who had now become his right arm for works of this nature, he found himself able to establish 'charities,' first in the parish of S. Saviour, then in that of S. Nicholas du Chardonnet, in which Louise resided. She revised and slightly modified the sets of rules for the use of the city. 'You are a splendid daughter,' wrote S. Vincent to her, ' to have thus adapted the rules of the charity and I thoroughly approve of it.'

Once introduced into Paris, the work never ceased to develop, and we shall see in a moment how this development brought about the beginning and in the end the organisation of the Sisters of Charity in the shape of a religious congregation. Louise de Marillac who naturally presided over the beginnings of her own parish ' charity,' that of S. Nicholas du

D

Chardonnet, spent herself lavishly on it with her usual ardour, never failing, in accordance with the prescription of the rule, ' to go in her turn to the poor, carrying " the soup-pot," ' that is to say, the pot containing food already cooked, and distributing its contents, ' serving the poor with her own hands ' as the rule laid down. This was all the more meritorious as plague was then raging in Paris and its victims were to be counted in thousands. Moreover, the hastily buried corpses were spreading the contagion. The Hôtel-Dieu alone, during these years, admitted every year more than eighteen hundred patients who had been attacked by the plague. Louise exposed herself to this scourge ; she braved contagion to nurse the sick and to visit the poor in their wretched dwellings with a simple courage and a Christian indifference that seemed to ignore danger and aroused the admiration of all who beheld her. S. Vincent, hearing of her bravery, could not refrain from writing to her : ' I confess, Mademoiselle, that this has so touched my heart that if night had not already fallen, I would have set off immediately to see you. But God's loving-kindness for those who give themselves to Him to serve the poor in the confraternity of charity in which, so far, no one has been attacked by the plague, has caused me to put the most perfect confidence in Him that you will suffer no harm thereby. . . . No, Mademoiselle, fear not. *Our Lord wishes to make use of you for something that concerns His glory, and I believe He will preserve you for it.*' The saint knew her too well to think of putting a check on her charitable activities, and, whilst urging her to take all necessary precautions, never dreamed for a moment of holding her back.

Towards the end of December of this year 1629, Louise de Marillac, despite her delicate health, paid a visit to the charity at Asnières. 'I set out,' she wrote in a report still preserved, 'on the Wednesday in the Quarter Tense of Advent, for Asnières, though I was afraid to undertake the journey on account of my physical weakness. However, I felt strengthened by the thought that I was going there out of obedience. At Holy Communion on that morning, I felt urged to make an act of faith, and this feeling remained with me for a very long time. It seemed to me that God would grant me health as long as I believed, contrary to all appearances, that He could give me this strength and I remembered how S. Peter's faith had enabled him to walk upon the waters. Lastly, during the whole of my journey, it seemed to me that I was acting without making any effort on my own part, and with much consolation seeing that it was God's will that I, unworthy as I am, was helping my neighbour to know Him.'[2] Two months later, in February 1630, Louise made a visitation of the confraternities at Saint-Cloud and Suresnes. Before setting out, she assisted at Mass and received Holy Communion from the hands of S. Vincent. This Communion marked a definite stage in the inner life of Louise, who was making constant progress in the highest ways of the spiritual life even when she seemed to be completely absorbed in exterior works and the practices of a life wholly devoted to the love of her neighbour in its manifold forms.

She has also noted, in order not to forget the fact, that it was on the anniversary of her wedding-day that she set out for Saint-Cloud.[3] ' I left for Saint-Cloud on the feast of S. Agatha, the 5th of February (1630). At Holy Communion, it seemed to me that our Lord inspired me with the thought of taking Him as the spouse of my soul, and even that this was now a sort of espousals. I felt much more strongly united to God by this thought, which was most unusual as far as I am concerned, and I had the idea of leaving all things to follow my Spouse, to regard Him as such in the future, and to endure whatever trials I might encounter as sharing with Him in all things. By God's permission, as I had a desire to have Mass celebrated that morning, for it was the anniversary of my marriage, and as I had abstained from doing so in order to perform an act of poverty, for I wished to be utterly dependent on God in the action I was about to perform, I said nothing about it to my confessor who celebrated the Mass at which I went to Communion. But when he arrived at the altar, it occurred to him to offer up the Mass for me and also to say a nuptial mass.' Thus strengthened and abandoning herself completely to the will of Him to whom she gave herself more fully every day, Louise set out on her new series of journeys. She visited the associations at Saint-Cloud and Suresnes in the most detailed fashion. She showed so much zeal at this work that S. Vincent, with a truly Christian solicitude, grew uneasy about her health, even though he was urging her on in the ways of perfection. He wrote to her on February 19th :[4]

' I praise God, Mademoiselle, that you have health enough for sixty of the people to whose salvation you have devoted yourself, but I beg you to let me know exactly whether your lungs have not been injured by having to speak so much, or your head on account of all the noise and worry.'

After Saint-Cloud, she went on to all the other confraternities in the environs of Paris, to Sannois, Franconville, Herblay, Conflans, and Villepreux, and inspected with the utmost care all the associations that had been established in these places. Everywhere she went she roused the zeal of the members, corrected any abuses or practices contrary to the true spirit of the work which, as always here below, may glide into the best enterprises and spoil the best intentions, if they be not carefully supervised and directed with unceasing vigilance. She worked so hard that her first biographer tells us she fell ill as a result. S. Vincent immediately hastened to obtain news of her and wrote :

' Blessed be God, Mademoiselle, that you are now better and that you have such a taste for labouring for the salvation of souls.[5] But I am very much afraid you are working too hard. . . .

' Take care of that, I beseech you, Mademoiselle. Our Lord wishes us to serve Him wisely and the contrary to that is called indiscreet zeal.'

During the whole of the remainder of this year, 1630, Louise de Marillac after short sojourns in Paris, continued to visit the environs of the capital, sometimes inspecting associations already established, sometimes founding new branches, but everywhere bestowing alms, training new members of the confraternity, distributing and explaining the rules of the 'aforesaid confraternities' which S. Vincent had by then modified. She did all this with the same courage and energy as she had shown from the first, spending herself, lavishing her person and property, in complete self-forgetfulness, but not always sufficiently careful about the preservation of her health and strength, despite the repeated warnings of her director. However, she never ceased from being 'very gay,' which he always advised her to be.

During Louise de Marillac's journeys up and down the country to visit all those charities which had already been established within a very brief space of time, she was able to observe their rapid development and constant progress. In Paris, things were not going quite so well, and S. Vincent, warned by his faithful fellow-worker, was not slow to realise that if the work there were to develop successfully, it was essential to introduce some modifications. In the country districts, the devoted women who joined the confraternities of Charity were in the main strong and healthy, quite accustomed to hard, manual labour, and moreover, the number of the poor and sick was relatively small. This was not so in the town, and especially in Paris. S. Vincent says so expressly in one of his Conferences :[6]

'The sick were badly looked after in these parishes, both on account of their large number and because the Ladies could not manage to go and serve them ; this was not feasible on account of their husbands and their household duties, and also because fathers and mothers were loath to give their daughters permission. Finally, things were not going well, because it was the will of God that there should be a Company of young women destined solely for the service of the poor under the control of the Ladies of Charity. . . .' 'In this city of Paris,' he says in another place,[7] 'some ladies had a desire to help the sick poor in their parishes. But when it became necessary to carry out such a useful project, they revolted, despite their good will, against rendering the sick the painful and humiliating services demanded of them.

' When I was going around giving missions, I met a good village girl who had given herself to God to teach the little girls around her. She was compelled, for good reasons, to abandon this work, and she then came to see me and I suggested to her to nurse the sick. She agreed at once, and I sent her to Saint Saviour's, which was the first parish in Paris in which the Charity was established. From Saint Saviour's it spread to S. Nicholas du Chardonnet and afterwards to S. Benedict's, where a number of other village girls had gathered together. God showered so many blessings on them that from that time onwards they began to live in community, and their numbers imperceptibly increased. In this way, my daughters, you see how the reason which S. Augustine gives us for ascertaining if certain works come from God is manifest in your community. If people ask you how it has come into existence, you may truthfully reply that you do not know.'

Mademoiselle Le Gras had also learned from personal experience and in the course of the journeys she had taken to visit the ' Charities,' of the usefulness, and in cities even the necessity of some permanent source of help for the Ladies.   This could only be effected by means of zealous persons who would devote themselves entirely to the work and who should have no other duties or preoccupations apart from it.   In Paris, as has just been said, it was absolutely indispensable if the undertaking were to succeed and bear fruit.   As there would have been a very reasonable repugnance against handing over such a work to mere paid servants, it was essential to have recourse to the religious zeal of ' the poor village girls ' referred to by S. Vincent.   In this way they became, unconsciously to themselves and also perhaps to Louise and S. Vincent, the first Sisters of Charity and the forerunners of that innumerable band which, we may say without exaggeration, has spread over the whole face of the globe.

Everything about the first attempts of this new association seems to have been so spontaneous, so little prepared, and in the very beginning even so unconscious, that it is difficult to assign an exact date and moment for its beginning.   Things seemed as if they were happening quite of themselves, one would be tempted to say, were it not that behind these occurrences lay the Divine Will which accomplishes all things without noise or confusion and can draw them as it were out of nothing.   Men were soon to see the hand of God at work and to have fresh proofs of how He is pleased to produce the greatest ends from the humblest beginnings and to bring forth the most wonderful results by the simplest of means.

Mademoiselle Le Gras herself had, in truth, on several occasions received offers of help from country girls who wished to live with her and assist her, but she received them into her home only for a time, and had no idea of keeping and training them to carry on works of charity. As it had now become perfectly clear that further help was required to enable the Ladies of Charity to continue, Louise came to the conclusion that she might unite her forces with some of these good ' village girls,' and though still without any definite design of permanently associating herself with them, or training them, she availed herself of their assistance and made use of them as fellow-labourers in her task. It was in February 1630 that Louise first made use of their services. The first of her associates was a young girl from the hamlet of Suresnes, whose name was Margaret Naseau, and who has earned the honour of being called the first Daughter of Charity.[8] ' As a matter of fact,' S. Vincent related many years afterwards, ' she was just a poor country girl who had scarcely any other teacher than God himself.' . . . ' She did not know how to read, and yet, as she had a strong inspiration from on high to teach the young, she bought an alphabet ; and as she could not go and present herself in the school, she stole off quietly at first to see the parish priest or the curate to ask them what were the first four letters, and then what were the next four, and so on for the remainder.

Afterwards, whilst she was minding her cows, she studied her lesson, and as soon as ever she saw anybody passing by who was able to read, she used to say: " Sir, how should that word be pronounced ? " And thus little by little she learned to read and then she taught the other girls of her village and after that made up her mind to go from village to village instructing the young. She won over both to herself and her mission two or three other girls whom she had taught to read ; they made a similar resolution and together with her they carried it out ; one girl in one village, another girl in another. And what is still more remarkable, she did all this without any money and with no help save that of Divine Providence. The result was that she had to fast sometimes for whole days and live in places where there was nothing but the bare walls. She sometimes spent the whole day and night instructing not only little girls but also grown women, and did all this without any vanity, self-complacency or other help than that of the grace of God, which provided for her chief needs without her ever giving a thought to them. She told Mademoiselle Le Gras that on one occasion she spent some days without food and without speaking to any one, but on coming home from assisting at Mass, she found enough to subsist on for quite a long time. The harder she worked at teaching the children, the more she was laughed at and calumniated by the villagers who were amazed to see her behaving in such a way, but this only served to increase her zeal to labour still harder. She was so utterly detached that she gave away

everything she possessed, and stinted herself of the
necessaries of life to give to others. . . .

' She provided for the education of some young
men, who had no means of doing so, feeding
them often enough and encouraging them to
serve God, and afterwards they became very good
priests.

' Finally, having heard that there was a confraternity in Paris for the sick poor, she felt herself
strongly urged with a desire to be employed in this
work so as to practise charity more perfectly. . . .
She came to see me and when I suggested this to her
she accepted it at once, and in this way she became
the first daughter of Charity.'

Such was Louise de Marillac's first assistant, and
it may easily be imagined that under her guidance,
Margaret rapidly became the most useful of her
fellow-workers. Shortly after Margaret Naseau's
reception, several other ' country girls ' joined,
attracted by her example. Vincent de Paul and
Louise de Marillac on their side, gathered together
a number of other devout young women, and thus
a little group of pious and charitable souls was
formed. They determined to consecrate themselves
entirely to the practice of good works, and were
employed either in the Paris ' charities ' or in
those of neighbouring towns in which extra help
and some permanent assistance had been found to
be essential. So far, this was all that had been
attempted, and none of them, neither the ' country
girls ' who were devoting themselves heart and soul
to the work, nor Vincent nor Louise dreamed of
doing anything further. S. Vincent de Paul, many

years later, painted a portrait of these first helpers of Mademoiselle Le Gras at one of the conferences he was accustomed to hold with the Sisters of Charity, and we cannot refrain from the pleasure of setting it down, so life-like and natural is it, and a portrait, as it were, by anticipation of the ' Sister of Charity ' as we all know her to-day. ' Real, true village girls,' he says, ' are extremely simple. They never make use of artifice or of words capable of bearing a double meaning. They are not self-opinionated or attached to their own ideas, and believe quite simply whatever they are told. . . . True humility may be remarked in a real village girl : they do not boast of their parentage ; they do not think themselves clever ; they act quite simply and frankly, and although some of them possess property, they are not conceited on that account and live just like the others. . . . The humility of good village girls—I repeat the word good—causes them to be without ambition. They are satisfied with what God has given them. They desire nothing else except food and clothing : their speech is humble and absolutely truthful. . . . They are extremely modest in their demeanour and in their dress which is rough and poor. . . . Can greater obedience be seen than that of really good village girls ? Do they not come home from their work, quite tired out and weary, to eat a frugal meal ? If the weather is favourable for work, and their fathers and mothers bid them go back to it, they do so without delay, and pay no attention to their weariness and their own arrangements.' Is not that a portrait of the Sister of Charity as she has shown herself for nearly three

centuries, devout, alert, gay, simple and kind,
ready for every form of good work, never tired and
never asking anything for herself ?

This first attempt at training a new sort of servant
of the poor, distinct from the Ladies of Charity and
completely devoted to good works of all kinds, was
made about this period, that is to say, about 1630.
It did not, as a matter of fact, absorb all Louise de
Marillac's energies, because notwithstanding her
usual delicate state of health, her activity only
increased the more she had to do. She continued
her unending visitations of associations that had
already been established, and strove to found new
ones. She devoted herself to this task with a zeal
that never grew colder but with the result that her
strength began to give way. In the autumn of this
year 1630, she went to Villiers-le-Bel and then on to
Beauvais, where, despite the opposition of a royal
procurator (which, indeed, subsequently proved to
be futile), ' charities ' had been established as far
back as 1627. Wherever she went she showed the
same zeal, teaching catechism to the children,
training catechists, who were a sort of schoolmistress intended to teach Christian doctrine, supervising the alms given to the poor by the Ladies of
Charity and the nursing of the sick ; spending herself
without rest and that to such a degree that she fell
ill again, and was compelled to call a halt. ' Is
there any remedy to cure you, Mademoiselle, seeing
that you have to talk so much and that the air is
keen and sharp and that you have a cold ? Surely,
if you do recover your health perfectly, it must be
said that God Himself cured you. I am waiting to

obtain fuller news about you to-day or to-morrow.'[9] However, thanks to her energetic will, which would brook no obstacles, she was soon on the high road to recovery and receiving from S. Vincent words of advice replete with an enlightened solicitude for the health of his fellow-worker as well as that modera- tion in well-doing which was so characteristic of his spirit.[10]   ' Has not your heart been deeply consoled at seeing how it has been found worthy before God of suffering by serving Him ? Certainly, you owe Him special thanks for that, and you should do your best to ask Him for the grace to make a good use of it.   Blessed be God that you are now quite well again and that the keenness of the air has not injured you ; as that is so, you will please continue until you have gathered almost as much fruit there as you have done elsewhere.   But if there is any symptom of a relapse, forestall it, please, and return here. . . .' A few days later he writes :[11] ' Blessed be God for your safe arrival in good health.   Take great care, therefore, to preserve it for the love of our Lord and his poor members, and be on your guard against doing too much.   That is a trick of the devil's by which he deceives devout souls by urging them on to do more than they can accomplish so that they may be unable to do anything at all, whereas the spirit of God gently incites one to do the good one reasonably can, so that one may continue doing it perseveringly and for a long time. Act then in this way, Mademoiselle, and you will be acting in accordance with the spirit of God.'[12] Louise de Marillac forced herself to follow the wise advice of her holy director, but her zeal was not of a nature

to be easily modified at will, and the fruits she was
gathering were so abundant from the very start
as to close, so to say, the mouth to all objections.
Hence when she left Beauvais, the confraternity of
Charity was established in the thirty-three parishes
of that city and its environs, as each of them desired
to have a branch of its own. ' Having learned,' her
first biographer tells us, ' of the honours rendered
her in this place, M. Vincent reminded her of the
union she should maintain with Jesus mocked and
humiliated.' He wrote to her, on December 4,
1630 :[13] ' When you are esteemed and honoured,
Mademoiselle, preserve a really true and humble
state of mind, as far as both honours and contempt
are concerned, and act like a bee which makes its
honey from the dew that falls on wormwood as
well as from that which falls on the rose.' She
looked on this advice, says her first biographer, as a
salutary precaution in the midst of the honours and
applause she received on her journeys. She made
use of these friendly dispositions only to promote
charitable works with more zeal and love than ever
wherever she went. She began, in the first place,
with meetings for ladies who came in large numbers
and were charmed by her addresses. As men were
not allowed to be present at these assemblies, they
entered the houses in which she gave her conferences and concealed themselves so as to hear without
being seen. They departed delighted and astonished.
' There were some,' as a Sister tells us later, ' who
even asked if she did not hear confessions.' ' When
she left Beauvais,' as the same chronicle tells us,
' the whole population accompanied her along the

roads calling down a thousand blessings and thanksgivings on her.'

' Now it happened that a child in the crowd fell underneath the wheel of her covered cart, which passed over the middle of its body ; she was profoundly moved by such an unfortunate accident, and having said some prayers, she saw the child arise without having received any hurt, and walk away with the greatest ease.'

Whilst Mademoiselle Le Gras was thus labouring with equal zeal and perseverance at the establishment of those ' charities ' which were to prove so productive of good, and exercising, without noise or general applause, such a constant and efficacious influence for good on all sorts of persons, her other work kept on developing. The little nucleus of ' good village girls ' whom she was training for all forms of charitable work, was also growing noiselessly, and so continuously from the very start as clearly to indicate its heavenly origin. Yet no one was more surprised at this than the foundress. Not indeed, as usually happens in these kinds of enterprises, that trials and contradictions were wanting to the new association. For instance, Margaret Naseau, of whom we have already spoken, the first helper whom it had given her so much pleasure to train, and who had quickly turned out to be her most valuable assistant, was carried off in 1631, the victim of her own devotion for the plague-stricken. This terrible scourge continued to ravage Paris, and indeed the whole of France, at this epoch, and rendered the people utterly terror-stricken, as we learn from contemporary accounts. The new ' servants of the poor ' were only too eager to nurse all who were attacked by the plague, and Margaret Naseau was even more eager than her companions. ' She had been attached to three different parishes in turn,' we are told, ' and had left each of them to the great regret of everybody, for they all loved her, and in truth there was nothing in her that was not lovable.'[14] ' Her charity,' said S. Vincent de Paul in one of his conferences, ' was so great right up to the end that she died from having placed a plague-stricken girl in her own bed. When she herself was attacked by this malady, she went off to the Saint Louis Hospital, her heart filled with joy and conformity to the will of God and bade good-bye to the Sister who was with her as if she knew quite well she was going to die.'[15] A few days later, in February 1631, Margaret Naseau passed away, a victim to her charity, and she has given us, as the first Sister of Charity, the model and type of what the true Sister of Charity has always been in succeeding centuries.

She was, as it were, the victim that was to consecrate and bring down God's blessing on the entire work. Neither did Mademoiselle Le Gras spare herself, for she tended the plague-stricken with her own hands and breathed the contaminated air with a tranquil courage very rare just then when the fear of contagion was wide-spread. If S. Vincent de Paul fully manifested his admiration for her, nevertheless he made no attempt to hold her back when ' it was a question of nursing the sick and labouring for the glory of God.'[16] ' Don't be afraid,' he wrote

E

to her, 'our Lord means to make use of you for
something or other in which His glory is concerned,
and I believe He will preserve you for that.'   And
yet it does not seem that, despite this sort of vision
of what the future held in store for his fellow-
worker, Vincent de Paul had at this time either a
full knowledge or intuition of it ; at least, he did
not wish to admit it, as we may see from a letter
he wrote in reply to one from Mademoiselle Le
Gras, who just then had expressed a desire to devote
herself completely to the service of God and of the
poor.   She wished to quit the world entirely, and
had even asked her spiritual guide to authorise her
to do so.[17]   ' I beseech you once for all,' he said to
her, ' not to think about it at all, until our Lord
clearly indicates His wishes, and just now, He is
inspiring me with sentiments contrary to your idea.
One desires to do many good things and it is a desire
that seems to be according to God ; nevertheless,
this is not always the case.   But God permits this
desire to prepare the mind for what He actually
wishes.   Saul was seeking for an ass, and found a
Kingdom : Saint Louis, for the conquest of the
Holy Land, and he gained a victory over self and a
crown in Heaven.   You are seeking to remain the
servant of these poor girls, and God wishes you to
serve Him and perhaps more people than you would
in this particular way.   And even if you were only
His servant, is not that enough ? For God's sake,
let your heart honour the tranquillity of our Lord's
heart, and it will be in a fit and proper spirit to serve
Him ! The Kingdom of Heaven is the peace of the
Holy Spirit ; It will reign in you if your heart is in

peace. Let it be so then, Mademoiselle, and you will honour in sovereign fashion the God of peace and love.' Mademoiselle Le Gras submitted, and waited peacefully for the moment fixed by Divine Providence. This example shows us how prudently and skilfully S. Vincent directed his penitent whose ardent soul was ever for pressing on, and who seems to have had a confused idea of the rôle which Providence had destined for ' the country girls ' who had now become the servants of the poor. If he moderated her ardent desires and was the first to give her an example, by putting his own favourite maxim into practice, of going forward day by day according to the holy Will of God, without seeking to peer into the future, he was very far indeed from discouraging her. ' Always honour,' he wrote to her,[18] ' the inaction and the hidden state of the Son of God. That is your centre and that is what He demands of you now, in future, and for ever ; if His divine Majesty does not let you know and in such a manner that you cannot be deceived, that He asks something else of you, do not think about it, and do not let your mind run on it, but refer all such matters to me. I will think for both of us about the matter. Rest assured that you will thus be in the state God demands of you whilst waiting to move you on to another for His greater glory, in case He judges it to be expedient.'

No doubt S. Vincent also desired, whilst thus maintaining Mademoiselle Le Gras in a state of expectancy and incertitude, to complete the task of training her in that complete detachment from self and even from the best and holiest things, which is demanded by Christian perfection, and which forms, as it were, its solid foundation. For even in Louise de Marillac's lively and constant thirst for all that is good, there was nevertheless a certain amount of anxiety and a fear of doing anything wrong, which might have injured her if they had been suffered to increase. Her spiritual guide wished at any price to eliminate this anxiety and nervousness before giving her leave, so to say, to devote herself entirely to the perfect life consecrated solely to the practice of charity. This tendency, then, to exaggerate obligations, in a word, to scrupulosity, revealed itself in her who was later to bequeath to her Daughters their characteristic note of simplicity and broadmindedness. Moreover, it was manifested by an uneasiness and anxiety, which, if not exaggerated, was at least too acute, about her son's education, for she never ceased from thinking about him and his future with all a mother's love. It was, as S. Vincent often reminded her in his letters, the only feature in her character that showed any trace of womanly weakness. 'What am I to say,' he wrote to her, 'about this excessive tenderness? Certainly, it does seem to me that you should strive before God to get rid of it, because it will only serve to disturb your mind and deprive you of that tranquillity which our Lord wishes to see in your heart. God does not desire you to be preoccupied about him save in a gentle and dependent manner.' Yet this did not prevent the kind and thoughtful saint from constantly sending news of her 'little Michel' to such a real true mother, and with a wealth of detail which reveals his kindness of heart and how thoroughly he understood the anxieties of her whom he was seeking to calm. 'Do not be uneasy,' he wrote to her about the boy, ' we are taking care of him. . . . I will see him myself, but I beg you, be at rest ; he is under the special protection of our Lord and of His holy Mother on account of the many gifts and offerings you have made of him. . . . It seems to me that his mind is expanding more and more. He is wise and gay with us here, and behaves in such a fashion as to edify us all. If this goes on, we shall have reason to praise God and to hope that he may be your consolation.'

But if Vincent de Paul wished to perfect the train-ing of Louise de Marillac in order to detach her from all things before allowing her to follow out all the inspirations of her zeal, the tragic events which, during these years, marked the collapse of the fortunes of the Marillacs, were also a living example to her, or, as we would say to-day, an 'object-lesson' much more efficacious than mere words. She knew how to profit by them with a docile heart notwithstanding her devotion to her family, and this rude lesson finished by detaching her from all earthly things. It is not possible for us to give here a detailed account of the fall of the Marillacs and of the sombre tragedy that ensued. The Marillac family, which, as we have said, was allied with that of the Queen Mother Marie de Medicis, was absolutely devoted to the defence of her cause and her interests. After ' the Day of the Dupes,' Richelieu, who saw formidable adversaries in the Marshal and the Chancellor de Marillac despite their fall, and who never forgave their

opposition to his own rise, treated them with the
utmost severity. Those members of the family
who were entrusted with functions at the Court
were banished from it, whilst Marshal de Marillac,
who with Schomberg and Condé, was successfully
commanding the army in Italy, was ruthlessly
removed from his post, treated as a criminal and
brought, heavily guarded, to France, where he was
imprisoned at Vincennes, and accused of pecula-
tion. The charge was never really proved, for it
could never have been established that he had
acted differently or more harshly than other Army
commanders of his time. The Marshal was tried
by two successive commissions chosen and nominated *ad hoc*, despite his appeal to Parliament, to
whose jurisdiction he had the right of appeal as a
Marshal of France. His appeal was not allowed,
and he was at length unanimously condemned to
death at Rueil, a castle of Richelieu's, in which the
commission had been sitting. The Marshal's wife
was not even allowed to go and throw herself at the
feet of the King or of the Cardinal, and was repulsed
with such harshness that she died of the shock
before the execution of her husband, which followed
immediately after his condemnation. During this
time, Michel de Marillac, the Chancellor and the
Marshal's brother, a man of such virtue and
integrity as to compel the esteem and admiration
even of his enemies, was compelled to hand over
the seals which had never seemed to him to be anything else than ' a heavy burden,' and was then
dragged from prison to prison, first to Évreux and
then to Lisieux, Caen, and Châteaudun in succession.

Michel de Marillac was kept in close confinement in all these places and regarded as a State criminal for two years, during which he gave the most admirable example of detachment and charity, preparing himself for death with a serenity and calmness that struck his contemporaries so forcibly that even the Memoirs of Richelieu and of his partisans have been forced to pay it homage.

The Chancellor devoted himself exclusively to preparing for death which he felt was close at hand, for his health, which had never been strong, was now daily growing worse. He employed his enforced leisure in exercises of piety and good works, one of which was his celebrated French translation of the *Imitation of Christ*, which became a classic and has been reprinted over and over again. Always calm and serene, never showing the slightest animosity or bitterness towards his enemies, and even going so far as to forbid any attack on Richelieu in his presence, Michel de Marillac, having lived as a sage, to borrow the expression of a modern historian, welcomed death with the joy of the saint who recognises in it the great liberator and the gate to true happiness. When the physician told him his last hour was at hand, ' Praised be God,' was his reply, ' I could not hear better news ; I am ready, and as there is no time to lose, let us set to work.' He then asked with the greatest calmness to receive the last sacraments and exhorted his friends to quietness and resignation. He received the last rites of the Church without for a moment showing any diminution of his peace of joy. ' *Jam non sum de hoc mundo*,' he repeated several times, ' *vado ad*

Patrem.' ' I am no longer of this world, I go to the
Father.' After receiving Extreme Unction with a
fervour that edified all who were present, Chancellor
de Marillac, without showing any sign of worry or
agitation, tranquilly resumed the work on which he
had hitherto been engaged, a *Treatise on Eternal Life*,
and literally died pen in hand. ' My sight is failing,'
he said, ' the writing seems to be double.' Then,
without agony or pain, and never ceasing from
prayer, he surrendered his spirit to God on the
morning of August 7, 1632, in such peace and calm
as to extort the admiration of his adversaries and of
his gaolers, who could not restrain themselves from
testifying to it. We may easily imagine the bitter
grief and anguish, the anxieties and distress, these
tragic events, which touched her so closely, produced in the heart of Louise de Marillac. She had
always remained deeply attached to her relations,
and neither marriage nor the open profession of
what was then called ' the devout life ' had ever
diminished her warmth of heart or her tender
solicitude on their behalf. We may see indications
of her anxiety and of the part she took in the misfortunes of the de Marillacs in her letters to S.
Vincent. True Christian as she was, she sought to
control her grief and to place everything at the foot
of the Cross, but she does not conceal her anguish
and sorrow ; and S. Vincent, who was kindness
itself, whilst exhorting her to courage and resignation, also recommends simplicity, sincerity, and a
filial abandonment to God, virtues so different from
an affected courage or stoicism which frequently
serve to conceal more hard-heartedness than true

firmness of mind. It was S. Vincent himself who told her of the death of Marshal de Marillac's wife, who had just succumbed to the emotions caused by the tragic disgrace of her husband. Mademoiselle Le Gras was deeply and tenderly attached to her, by the common bonds of piety and devotion and a charitable love of the poor. ' Madame la Maréchale de Marillac,' S. Vincent wrote to her, ' has gone to Heaven to receive the reward of her labours. Well now, that will grieve you, but consider that as our Lord has so willed it we should adore his Divine Providence and strive to conform ourselves in all things to his holy Will, and indeed I know very well that your dear heart does not ask for anything better, and even if the inferior part is troubled and disturbed, it will soon grow calm. The Son of God wept for Lazarus. Why should you not weep for the dear woman ? There is no harm in that, provided that, like the Son of God, you conform yourself in all this to the Will of his Father, and that, I feel certain, is just what you will do.'[19]

On the tragic death of the Marshal, S. Vincent, thinking no doubt that the grief caused by such a catastrophe could not be consoled by mere words, but only by divine Grace, wrote simply :

' What you tell me of Marshal de Marillac seems to me deserving of the most profound sympathy, and deeply distresses me. Let us honour in this event the good pleasure of God and the happiness of those who honour the death of the Son of God by their own. It does not matter to us how our relations go to Heaven provided they arrive there. . . . Let us not grieve for him, and let us acquiesce in the adorable Will of God.'[20]

If S. Vincent was far from forbidding her to grieve, nevertheless, as he was somewhat mistrustful of Louise de Marillac's ardent spirit, and knew men better than she, he advised her to hold herself aloof from all these public disturbances and from the more or less useless proceedings they entailed. Having heard that Mademoiselle Le Gras was anxious to bring influence to bear on some distinguished personages of her acquaintance on behalf of the Chancellor, S. Vincent, who was well aware of the futility of such attempts in an affair in which almost only political interests were involved, suggested to her to let the matter rest.[21]   'As for M. de Marillac,' he writes, 'I approve of whatever you think is right ; but take care not to embarrass yourself in any way. It seems to me that, in such matters, one should be prepared to take the advice given by whomsoever one may consult, and when you have been advised to do something contrary to your own feelings, it is not well to return again to the matter. However, do whatever our Lord may suggest to you.   There is one thing of which I can perfectly assure you and that is He will never give you anything but perfect advice.'   If S. Vincent thus counselled Louise de Marillac not to take any part in political matters that did not directly concern her, and in which she could effect no result, he by no means forbade her to show her sympathy and affectionate concern for the misfortunes that touched her so closely. It has been suggested that she was the lady from Paris who went to visit the Chancellor,

then imprisoned at Châteaudun, and who was
refused admittance by the goaler, as stated in the
prison register.

A passage from a letter written in 1632 and
addressed to Mademoiselle Le Gras by her spiritual
guide, would seem to refer to this incident, though
the matter has never been fully cleared up. ' Hence
it would be better, Mademoiselle, to act as you
have informed me and to defer the business so as to
run no risk. But if, before my return from here,
you should meet some trustworthy person, do so ;
if not, defer it. Our Lord will provide, especially
if you really and truly love to remain at the foot of
the Cross where you are at present and which is the
best place in the world for you to be. So, love to
remain there, Mademoiselle, and fear nothing.'[22]
Saint Vincent de Paul was so far from wishing to
render her insensible to the trials of her family and
to separate her from it, that we find him in another
letter written in 1632, some weeks after the execution
of Marshal de Marillac, urging her to pay a visit
to the Castle of Attichy where some of the Marillac
family had assembled, still plunged in grief, and hot
with anger and resentment. Amongst others there
was the lovely Anne d'Attichy, well known afterwards as the Countess de Maur, who vowed eternal
hatred against Richelieu and who even refused
subsequently to receive Madame de Combalet, his
niece, who had asked to meet her, as she could not
make up her mind to receive the niece of her uncle's
murderer. In the midst of all this rage and grief,
the gentle figure of Louise must have appeared as a
messenger of peace and love, dressing the wounds

of the spirit with the same light and sure touch that she so well knew how to employ on the wounds of the body. S. Vincent let us see this when he wrote to Louise to encourage her to pay a visit to the unhappy family at Attichy, and to lay aside all scruples about doing so.

' It is not a purposeless visit to go and see the person who has asked you to go, and who is, perhaps, in need of your advice to make up her mind about something that may turn out to be excellent. So go then, Mademoiselle, go in the name of our Lord and with his blessing.'[23]

All these terrible catastrophes had ruined the fortunes of the Marillacs in a moment. Mademoiselle Le Gras took her share in them like a Christian and a Marillac, and they in no way interfered with her zeal in doing good. It was at this time, and this is a remarkable fact inasmuch as it shows us to what an extent she had even then devoted herself entirely to God and to good works, and how replenished her soul was with that divine Grace whose effects nothing can hinder and which trials only render more fruitful, it was then, we repeat, that the first association, which was destined to be the germ of the Society of the Daughters of Charity, took definite shape. Its foundation has even been assigned to this year. As a matter of fact, it was on November 29, 1633, in a small house in the old Rue des Fossés-Saint-Victor, now 43 Rue Cardinal Lemoine, that, without noise or ceremony, as usual under S. Vincent's direction, four of five of those ' good country girls ' who were to be the founda-tions of the Congregation and the first Sisters of

Charity, grouped themselves around Louise de Marillac.

The ' Charities ' continued, in point of fact, to develop in a manner that far exceeded the hopes of the founders, and the only explanation they gave of it was that it was due to a quite especial grace of Providence. But at the same time, the defects and weaknesses of the undertaking daily made themselves more and more felt. The want of unity of government, and the lack of training of the ' simple village girls,' who were intended gradually to replace in cities the Ladies of Charity who were prevented by their society engagements from devoting themselves wholly to good works, or whose zeal had grown cold ; and, in country districts, the mothers of families with households to look after, clearly showed the co-founders the absolute necessity of establishing something new. It was intended to serve as a centre and as a means of carrying on all the other works, whilst at the same time constituting a framework for the employment and utilisation of an army of charitable souls filled with good will and Christian devotedness. Without this, everything was bound to go to pieces, to vanish, as it were, in smoke, and once the ' first fine, careless rapture ' had passed, and the holy pioneers removed by death, which could not be long delayed, nothing would remain but wreckage, uncompleted beginnings which themselves would not be slow to disappear. Mademoiselle Le Gras seems to have been the first to see the absolute necessity of adopting a new line, or at least S. Vincent allowed her to express her ideas on the subject first, keeping himself as usual in the background. The letters of Vincent de Paul and of Louise de Marillac on this matter are most interesting and give us an admirable idea of their two characters. With this idea in mind we shall now give a few brief selections from the letters, for it seems to us to be of little import to try to discover whether the idea of the Congregation of the Daughters of Charity first occurred to Saint Vincent or to Louise. It is of slight importance whether the idea first occurred to him or to her or to both at the same time. What really does matter is that both of them, aided by Divine Grace, succeeded in realising their plan in the course of those years which were so fruitful in France for the religious life and for the enterprises that proceed from it. That is the crucial point, the one which it is useful for us to know, and which deserves to be placed in a clear light.

As Louise de Marillac had had the opportunity of seeing at close quarters the inconveniences which resulted both from a lack of training and from a lack of direction of the first servants of the poor, she had wished two years previously, as we have already observed, to consecrate herself entirely to the poor and to devote herself by vow to serve and instruct them, whilst at the same time renewing her vow of perpetual widowhood which she had taken on the death of her husband. But S. Vincent, calm as ever, had restrained her, telling her to wait in patience and humility, ' in the situation that befits a dear daughter of God.' But he had never forbidden her to think about a more or less distant future when she would be free to follow her desires in accordance with the mysterious will of Divine Providence, ' for the greater glory of God, in case he deems it expedient.' Two years later, the difficulties and want of co-ordination in a work that had only just started, so to say, became daily more visible. Mademoiselle Le Gras herself was suffering from her anomalous position in society, for malicious rumours were being circulated that she had had proposals of marriage and had accepted them. This rumour touched her to the quick and she regarded it as an insult. Hence S. Vincent believed that the moment had arrived to give her permission to follow out her inclination, and to form the nucleus of a ' little society,' as he said later, of which she should be the first Superior, even before there were any members or a Superior.

On November 29, 1633, as has been said, Louise de Marillac, with the express authorisation of S. Vincent de Paul, took up her residence in the Rue des Fossés-Saint-Victor with four or five almost uncultured poor girls, and set to work to train them for their mission of charity with a truly Christian zeal and joy. This was, in truth, the mysterious mustard-seed which by God's grace was to grow into such a great tree. Mademoiselle Le Gras was certainly delighted at now being able to devote herself wholly and for ever to God and to labour for his glory, yet she seems to have experienced a momentary attack of apprehension and a profound sentiment of her own inability to carry out such a task worthily. Such struggles are a clear revelation both of her deeply rooted Christian sentiments and of her faith, and they serve to show to what heights she had reached on the road to perfection. She wrote, in a notebook that has been preserved,[24] in regard to this memorable moment in her life :

'O my Lord, I have experienced an unutterable new light on the uncommon love Thou desirest from those creatures on whom Thou hast chosen in this world to exercise Thy love in its purity. Behold us here, a little band ; may we aspire to it ? It seems to me, indeed, that we have this desire in our hearts, but the knowledge of our weakness, owing to our past infidelities, leads us to fear lest Thou mayst reject us. Nevertheless, the memory of the fact that Thou didst not limit the number of times we should forgive our enemies, leads us to think that Thou wilt act in a similar way towards us, and as this is so, we believe we love Thee. . . . Thou truly lovest us, since Thou art one with the Father who has willed to show His love for us by giving Thee, His Son, to us. And we feel assured that Thou dost desire that we too should love Thee, since Thy law, both the Old and the New, commands it, and since Thou hast promised that we shall be loved by Thy Father, that Thou wilt come to us with Thy Father and abide in us if we love Thee. . . . Oh ! pure love, how I love Thee ! Since Thou art as strong as death, separate all that is contrary to Thee in me. . . . Behold us then, O my Lord, at the foot of Thy cross to which I see Thee fastened, that we may be drawn to Thee as Thou hast promised.'

Like everything else that is in accordance with the designs of Providence, the modest and obscure beginnings of Louise de Marillac's enterprise, about which we have such few details, soon began to develop to such a degree as to surprise everybody, and its authors more than all.

'The little snowball,' as S. Vincent said in his picturesque language which recalls that of S. Francis de Sales, grew so rapidly as to become visible to all who witnessed its unexpected development, of which God was the principal author and in which, to employ S. Vincent's expression again, 'God alone was everything.' Hence he offered no further objections to the ever-increasing zeal and ardour of Mademoiselle Le Gras, who devoted herself entirely to the training of a few girls, the first recruits in the Army of Charity. Nevertheless, the work was difficult, and at times even arduous, because the young girls or the widows whom she had to train, came from very different classes of society; some of them were of a rather rough type and had to be taught everything. But good-will and the love of God in our neighbour were not wanting and made up for everything else. As for Louise herself, she superabounded in joy; this indeed was the state of which God had formerly let her have a glimpse without her understanding how it could be realised.

Hence S. Vincent, seeing in her utterly disinterested ardour in which there was no trace of self-seeking, an evident sign of the Divine Will, gave her permission to consecrate herself entirely by a definite vow to this work to which God had so clearly called her. The first biographer of Mademoiselle Le Gras,[25] simply says with regard to this capital point in her life: 'Having undertaken the charge of

F

this new company, Mademoiselle Le Gras experienced so much love for her vocation that she desired to devote herself to it entirely. Accordingly, on March 25 of the following year, 1634, the feast of the Annunciation of our Lady, she bound herself to it by an irrevocable vow, and also renewed her vow of perpetual widowhood. And from that time on, she offered to God during her whole life one of her Communions every month in thanksgiving for having called her to this state.' This date, March 25, is a red-letter day with the Sisters of Charity and on it they renew their annual vows. The work, in fact, had come into existence and its founders were almost unconscious of it. They were as far removed from having any idea of its marvellous growth and of its wonderful value to the Church and the poor as they were from any pretentions to founding it. It now remains for us to see how the seed went on developing and how Louise de Marillac, constantly assisted and guided by S. Vincent de Paul, set about the organisation of her little community ; we shall see at the same time how her spiritual life kept on widening and deepening, now that she was definitely and permanently separated from the world.

NOTES ON CHAPTER II

[1] *Letters of S. Vincent de Paul to S. Louise de Marillac*, No. XI. p. 14,

[2] *S. Louise de Marillac, Thoughts and Writings*, p. 124.

[3] *Op. cit.*, p. 124.

[4] *Letters of S. Vincent de Paul*, No. XVII, p. 23.

[5] *Op. cit.*, No. XIX, p. 26.
[6] *Conferences of S. Vincent de Paul*, No. XXI, p. 96.
[7] *Op. cit.*, No. XVIII, p. 83.
[8] *Op. cit.*, No. XVI, p. 71.
[9] *Letters of S. Vincent de Paul*, No. XX, October 22nd, 1630, p. 28.
[10] *Op. cit.*, No. XX, October 22nd, 1630, p. 29.
[11] *Op. cit.*, p. 29.
[12] *Op. cit.*, No. XXIV, December 4th, 1630, p. 32.
[13] *Op. cit.*, No. XXIV, p. 35.
[14] Baunard, *op. cit.*, p. 128.
[15] *Conferences of S. Vincent de Paul*, No. XXVI, p. 72.
[16] Abelly, *op. cit.*, Bk. I, p. 146.
[17] *Letters of S. Vincent de Paul*, No. LX, 1631, p. 60.
[18] *Op. cit.*, No. XIII, p. 17.
[19] *Op. cit.*, No. XXXV, p. 51.
[20] *Op. cit.*, No. XLVIII, p. 69.
[21] *Op. cit.*, No. XLIX, p. 71.
[22] *Op. cit.*, No. LVI, p. 80.
[23] *Op. cit.*, No. LI, p. 73.
[24] S. Louise de Marillac, *Thoughts and Writings*, p. 66.
[25] Gobillon, *op. cit.*, p. 44.

CHAPTER III

'HAVE courage, my daughters,' S. Vincent[1] said to the first Sisters of Charity, 'and reflect on the mercy God has shown you by choosing you to be the first members of your Company. When Solomon resolved to build God's temple, he placed precious stones in the foundations to show that what he desired to do was most excellent.

'God in his goodness wishes to grant you, who are the foundations of this Company, the grace of being eminent in virtue. For I am sure that you would not wish to inflict an injury on those who come after you; and, as trees bring forth fruit only in accordance with their nature, there is every likelihood that those who come after you will not aim at a higher degree of virtue than what you will have practised. If God, then, has been pleased to give his blessing to this good beginning, strive then to be all the more virtuous.'

Hereupon all the Sisters declared that they wished to put into practice all that had been said to them, and also to observe the rule. All, including S. Vincent, then knelt down, and he continued as follows: 'May God in His goodness be pleased to imprint on your heart what I, a wretched sinner, have said to you on His behalf, so that you may be able to remember it easily in order to put it into practice, and to be true Daughters of Charity.   Amen.'

These words, which bring to a conclusion S. Vincent de Paul's first conference to the Daughters of Charity, would seem to contain the programme of the mission which God had entrusted to Louise de Marillac, and also to indicate the means of carrying it into effect.   The object of the enterprise attempted by the pious widow and her first imitators and companions was to strive to become more perfect so that they might be able to accomplish greater things and to become more holy so that they might be able to do more good to all around them.   We shall see how well she knew how to grasp the meaning of her work and how admirably she carried it out.

The word indeed increased rapidly in a century in which events moved more slowly than they do now.   In this respect it did not seem to fall in with S. Vincent's ideas, for he had no great liking for all things that move too quickly without taking time to profit by the experiences and lessons that years alone can give.   Moreover, both Vincent de Paul and Louise de Marillac, with that power of discrimination and certainty of vision characteristic of those who establish works destined to endure, were far more concerned about the worth of those who presented themselves for the work than about their number ;   and indeed they both showed themselves very strict in their selection.   But whilst carefully eliminating all those who did not seem to be qualified to carry out what was asked of them, or who did not give sufficient evidence of an ability to persevere, nevertheless they soon found themselves at the head of a little community of 'servants of the poor.' It was essential to train them, to guide their first steps in a path not only new to themselves but also to those who saw them at work, and this very fact only rendered the task all the more difficult. The necessity of a code of rules and regulations soon made itself felt, and despite the care that had been taken to avoid the slightest appearance of a new foundation, the very nature of things compelled them to make up their minds to draw up a set of rules and to put them in writing, if they were to guide the new arrivals and to undertake new establishments, for these too were multiplying much more quickly than might have been expected. S. Vincent, ever mistrustful of self and ever inclined to refer all matters to God's goodness, did not urge Louise de Marillac to compose a rule; quite the contrary, when she asked him to do so and told him that the community was suffering from being left without a code of rules, he replied :[2] 'Providence is treating you in this matter as it once did the people of God, who were left from the Creation for more than a thousand years without a law. Our Lord acted in the same way towards the early Church, for whilst he remained on earth, it had no written law, and it was only the Apostles, after His death, who gathered together His teachings and ordinances. . . . So I have not yet been able to make up my mind to put down in writing a code of rules for your house. . . .' 'Our Lord,' he wrote in another letter, 'has given the law of grace to men without

writing it down ; let us act in a similar fashion, at
least for some time.'³

When necessity at last compelled him to make a
move, S. Vincent de Paul chanced to be ill and
overwhelmed with work of every description,
hence he handed over the business to Louise de
Marillac and took no share in it ; in fact, she was not
even able to consult him. ' God wishes it so,' he
wrote to her, ' so that I may not place my sickle
in your harvest.'⁴ Louise de Marillac obeyed and,
probably in the early month of 1634, drew up a
short set of rules which was really little more than
an order of day. This regulation has been preserved and still serves as the basis of the rules of the
Sisters of Charity. These few perfectly simple and
practical rules were suggested by the experience she
had already acquired of the various needs of the
rising congregation. Hence, when she communicated this ' order of day ' to S. Vincent, the latter
sent it back accompanied by a few remarks which
must have seemed, coming from his hands, a real
recompense. ' I am sending you back the rules for
the Daughters and they are so good that I have
nothing to add ; read it to them at once, provided
you do not think I should be present ; in which
case, I firmly promise you that it will be one of the
first things I shall do on my return, if God so pleases.
It would be well if the Sisters of this parish were
present at the same time, in order that they may act
like the others.'

The meeting to which the saint refers took place
on July 31, 1634. The words pronounced by the
holy priest, when reading and commenting on the

provisional set of regulations drawn up by Mademoiselle Le Gras, were carefully written down
by those present, and form the first of those admirable conferences which constitute the rich source
from which Sisters of Charity imbibe the spirit of
their institute. He passes in review all the points
of the set of rules and explains them to the dozen
poor, attentive and deeply affected girls who were
listening to him. Beginning with the hour for rising
which was at first fixed for five o'clock and then on
account of the needs of the Sisters' work, altered to
four, S. Vincent goes on to the hour fixed for vocal
and mental prayer. Here he gives expression to the
love that filled his heart and cries aloud : ' Oh !
my daughters, this is the very centre of devotion.
God gives us a regular flood of holy thoughts during
prayer. It is said of the Blessed Virgin that she
treasured up in her heart the holy thoughts she had
gathered from the words of our Lord so that she
might nourish her soul on them, and the same is
true of Saint Magdalen at the feet of our Divine
Saviour ; following their example, my daughters,
gather them up carefully, and you will rejoice the
heart of God. Yes, if you do this you will be the
joy of God, and all the saints will rejoice thereat. . . .
Do not be afraid that poor uneducated girls, as you
think you are, cannot aspire to mental prayer. Oh !
God is so good ! And amongst the numerous
proofs He has given you of His goodness do not
forget that He has willed to call you to the practice
of charity. After that, how could you imagine He
would refuse you the grace you need for prayer.
Oh, my daughters, such an idea should never enter

your minds. I was greatly edified to-day, when talking to a young village girl like yourselves, who by her assiduity in prayer is now one of the holiest souls I know.'

The whole instruction, which is too long to be given here in full, is marked by that tone of simplicity which harmonises so admirably with the growing warmth and animation that reaches the heights of the truest and most moving eloquence. Point by point, S. Vincent analyses Mademoiselle Le Gras' code of rules which, as expounded by him, is raised to a higher plane and becomes a fervent exhortation to a greater advance in perfection. Speaking of patience and gentleness when dealing with the poor and sick, he said to them :[5] 'Bear with their little humours ; never get angry with them or say harsh words to them' ; then, growing more animated, S. Vincent cried out : ' Ah ! my daughters, they have enough to put up with in their misfortunes. Think, on the contrary, that you are their angel-guardians, their fathers and mothers : do not go against their wishes save in whatever might be harmful to them, because in such a case it would be cruel to give them what they ask for. Weep with them. . . . God has brought you into existence to console them.'

In her rule Mademoiselle Le Gras had set apart certain times for reading and study, and S. Vincent, with a presentiment of the future, returns with insistence to this point : 'Apply yourselves,' he told the Sisters,[6] ' to learning how to read, not for your own satisfaction and utility, but so as to render yourselves able to teach little girls in those places where they will be sent to you. How do you know what Providence intends to do with you? So, always hold yourselves ready to go where holy obedience may send you.' He then exhorted them to obey their superiors and to respect the Ladies of Charity. 'Also honour the sick,' he said, 'and look upon them as your masters.' When he went on to develop the fruits and advantages, both for the poor and for themselves, that might result from their labours, he added the following words which must have touched the hearts of Louise de Marillac and her companions, and kindled a desire for a complete observance of the few rules he was explaining to them : 'If there is anybody in the whole world who may hope for Paradise, is it not you? Why? Because, by observing this rule, you are sure to be doing the holy Will of God. The second fruit (of this observance) is that you are beginning a work which may go on for ever. Yes, my daughters, if you begin to observe your rule with the design of carrying out God's most holy Will, there is every reason to hope that your little community will last and increase. So be very much on your guard then, lest, if relaxation creeps in, it may be no less a matter than the abandonment of a good which God had willed from all eternity should exist, because it was for that end he chose you. Oh ! what a happiness for you, my daughters, if you act according to God's good pleasure ! Then your community will not only last for a time, but will continue doing the same good after you are dead, and this will be a reason for increasing your glory in Heaven.'

Then, after recommending humility and a sense of

their own littleness and lowliness, S. Vincent exhorted them to have an invincible, unshakable confidence in the help of Divine Providence, as far as their material needs were concerned.[7] 'For one crown, you will have a hundred, for one home, a hundred, for one family, a hundred, so that Providence will never fail you. . . . So now, my daughters, what have you to be afraid of ? Has not God entered into a covenant by which He guarantees that those who care for the poor will never want for anything ? Hence, love the promise of your God more than all the treasures of this world.' Mademoiselle Le Gras and her little flock, deeply moved by the saint's words and full of ardour, knelt down, and each of those present protested her good will and loyalty. Then S. Vincent, who was also much moved, exhorted them once more to perseverance, and one cannot read without emotion the concluding words of this discourse which we have already given. The whole conference, indeed, is replete with that communicative warmth which springs from interior zeal and profound convictions. S. Vincent's soul in all its greatness is revealed in his words, and one can easily imagine the impression they must have produced on those who heard them falling from his lips. 'After which,' as the report of this first conference states, with charming simplicity, 'each of the sisters went back to her work.'

The remembrance of this first conference has remained dear to the Sisters of Charity who frequently re-read it. As a matter of fact, the care S. Vincent took to point out clearly the manner of accomplishing their mission 'of true Daughters of

Charity,' in the best possible manner, indicates that this was the definitive extablishment of their 'little company.' But if Vincent de Paul and Louise de Marillac had even a vague presentiment of the great work that had just begun and of its fruitfulness, they did not reveal it either by word or by action.

They followed with docility the indications of the Divine Will and referred all else to God's good pleasure. Some years later, when the work had made surprising progress, Saint Vincent repeated the same idea to his Daughters in a discourse which he pronounced on January 6, 1642.[8] He said, with his usual simplicity : ' Make no mistake about it ; it is God alone who has created your company. It is He, yes, my daughters, it is He who has chosen you, and who has made you all that you are : we never had any definite design in this matter. Who would ever have thought that there would be Daughters of Charity when the first of them arrived to serve the poor in a few parishes in Paris ? Oh, my daughters ! I never even thought of it, neither did your Sister Servant, nor Fr. Portail : so then it was God who thought of it, and hence we may say it is He who is the author of your Company, for we cannot in truth discover any other. Oh ! blessed be God ! that you are indebted to His bounty for having been chosen, though poor village girls, to form a company which, aided by His grace, will serve Him faithfully. And what foundation do you think our Lord left for the establishment of His Church ? Only twelve men, His apostles, all of whom were put to death. Oh ! how different are the works of

God from those of men ! . . . No, my daughters,
do not fear. God will never fail you, if you are
faithful to Him. So then set to work courageously
to make yourselves perfect in serving the poor.'

If the founders of this ' little Company ' thus
refused, in the most sincere humility, to claim the
honour of having done so, the world, which saw
them at work, was not so reserved and did not fail
to attribute it to them. From all sides came help
and co-operation, and also appeals for their devoted
care and experience. This double movement, which
supplied the enterprise with both the means and
the opportunity of development, surprised Louise
de Marillac and her wise director more than
anybody else ; but with their customary simplicity
and humility they devoted themselves to the work
without anxiety or hesitation and obeyed with
equal joy and submission what was so evidently
the holy Will of God. Louise de Marillac, who had
been a well-known figure in the fashionable world
of Paris of her time, before she completely devoted
herself to works of charity, had kept up a large
circle of acquaintances, with the result that many
of her friends regarded it as a duty to assist her, and
gladly turned to her for help and advice. S. Vincent,
on his side, introduced her to the ' Ladies of
Charity ' who cheerfully placed themselves under
her guidance, and sought to do as much good as they
could in their own spheres of action.

Hence the names of Madame de Miramion, so
celebrated in the annals of charity of that period,
Madame de la Chassaigne, Madame de Herse,
Madame de Gondi, mother of the celebrated

Cardinal de Retz; Madame Pollalion; Mademoiselle Viole; Madame Séguier, wife of the Chancellor; Madame Fouguet, mother of the future Superintendent of Finance; the Duchess of Ventadour, who became one of Louise de Marillac's most loyal friends; the Duchess of Liancourt before her open profession of Jansenism had compelled Mademoiselle Le Gras to break off all intercourse with her, and many other famous names constantly recur in Louise de Marillac's letters as active and devoted fellow-workers in all her charitable enterprises.

Two names, however, are mentioned so frequently as to deserve a special commemoration, and these are Madame Goussault, wife of the President of that name, and Madame de Combalet, niece of Cardinal Richelieu, who has remained celebrated in the history of charity of those days under the name of the Duchess of Aiguillon. The latter is too well known to allow us to dwell very much on this gracious and lovable niece of the unbending Cardinal. She was beautiful, wealthy, and even powerful through the influence she exercised over her uncle, but she despised all earthly goods to devote herself entirely to God and to works of charity. She had been prevented by Cardinal Richelieu from carrying out her wish to become a Carmelite nun in the convent that had just been founded by Madame Acarie, and she now lived in society and at Court as if dwelling in a foreign land, giving good example in the fullest sense of the term, where it was so badly needed, devoting all her spare time and all her wealth to good works of every description, under the advice

and direction of S. Vincent de Paul who introduced
her to all his charitable undertakings, and brought
her into touch with Louise de Marillac.

Souls who resembled each other so closely in
their love of God and of his poor, in contempt of
the world and in nobility of ideas, were so well
adapted to understand each other that there was
little delay before a close friendship and intimacy was
established between them, though everything might
have seemed to fix a gulf between the niece of
Cardinal Richelieu and the niece of Marshal de
Marillac. Hence we shall see Madame de Combalet
(afterwards, the Duchess of Aiguillon) always side
by side with Mademoiselle Le Gras, assisting her
both with her credit and money, her time and
labour, and one of the first to understand and to
support the creation of the Daughters of Charity.
Her name appears at every meeting at which the
resolutions were taken that decided the existence
and the permanence of the work ; we shall see her
aiding the extablishment by her credit and helping
on the extension of the first Sisters of Charity. So
much did she appreciate the Sisters and the services
they rendered the poor, that two years after their
establishment, she asked for a sister to come and
live with her in order to help her in her own private
acts of charity. Saint Vincent did not think he
could refuse and appointed a Sister named Marie
Denyse[9] to the post. ' But,' as he wrote to Louise
de Marillac, ' she gave me a reply worthy of a
daughter called by God to practise charity ; she
said she had left her father and mother to give
herself to the service of the poor for the love of

God, and begged me to excuse her if she could not alter her decision and go and assist this great lady.' Another Sister named Barbara Angiboust, one of Louise de Marillac's ablest assistants in the beginning, whose name is constantly mentioned in the early annals of the Company, showed herself more docile at first, but scarcely had she reached the Palace of the Petit Luxembourg, where Madame de Combalet was then living, than she took fright at finding herself amidst such surroundings, ' utterly astonished at the sight of such a splendid court,' and she went off weeping to S. Vincent, begging him to ' take her away from it.' Our Lord, she said, had given her to the poor, and it was the poor alone she wished to serve and to whom she desired to be sent back. Her request was granted after a few days' delay, and Madame de Combalet had to content herself with going to the Sisters of Charity in their own home to obtain their assistance. ' What do you think of that ? '[10] wrote Vincent de Paul to Mademoiselle Le Gras, ' are you not delighted to see the strength of the spirit of God in these two poor girls, and the contempt of the world and its grandeurs which it has inspired in them ? You cannot imagine what courage it has given me for the work, or the desire I feel for your speedy return in good health so that you may work at it with a right good will.' We may see from the very beginning, how the disciples of Louise de Marillac were even now what the future was so clearly to reveal them, solely devoted to God and His poor.

The other figure to be seen side by side with Louise de Marillac from the earliest days of the new

enterprise is that of Madame Goussault. Geneviève
Fayet married Anthony Goussault, First President
of the Court of Exchequer, and in 1631 was left a
widow with the difficult task of bringing up five
children. Very wealthy, beautiful and witty,
Madame Goussault, as Abelly tells us in his quaint
style, ' possessing all the qualities and all the gifts
of nature and of grace, might still have aspired to
great connections in the world. But she generously
renounced all such ideas to consecrate herself to
the poor, and especially to the sick.'[11] Madame
Goussault, with her lively and somewhat impetuous
character, her numerous connections with the best
society of Paris, with the nobility and the judiciary,
was a most valuable recruit for the task undertaken
by S. Vincent de Paul who appreciated her worth
immediately, and in 1628 introduced her to Louise
de Marillac.

Between these two women, who resembled each
other in so many respects, the most intimate and
affectionate relations were rapidly established.
Madame Goussault, without neglecting for a moment her duties as a mother and the mistress of a
great house, gave both Vincent de Paul and Mademoiselle Le Gras the most generous and most active
assistance, to such a degree indeed that her name
deserves to be joined with theirs from the very
beginning of the undertaking and cannot be passed
over in silence if we wish to be true to history.
She devoted her attention to the various new
' charities ' that were being formed, secured new
recruits for the Ladies of Charity, and supervised
the functioning of the work both in Paris and in

G

the provinces. S. Vincent sent her even as far as Angers, where she had estates, and she accomplished her mission everywhere with a zeal that was only equalled by her joyful energy.

As gay and as amiable in the smallest village as she might have been in the most brilliant society of the capital, she devoted her attention particularly to primary schools, in which the Daughters of Mademoiselle Le Gras, from the very start, and in conformity with the spirit of their rules, worked ceaselessly and courageously. But Madame Goussault, or rather 'the President' as she was usually called, was especially attracted to visiting the sick in the hospitals which were at that time poorly and badly kept. Imitating the example of Louise de Marillac who visited and from the very beginning took her daughters with her to visit those who were sick in hospital, Madame Goussault diligently attended the various hospitals of Paris, and no matter where she travelled, made a point of visiting the local hospital when there was one. It was she who induced S. Vincent to give permission to the Ladies of Charity to visit the great hospital of the Hôtel-Dieu, which they were eager to do, and to lend the assistance of the Sisters of Charity. This soon became one of their most important occupations in Paris.

The Hôtel-Dieu, the foundation of which went back to the rise of the French monarchy, and which had recently been enlarged, admitted twenty to twenty-five thousand patients a year.

Despite the efforts of the Augustinian nuns who had recently been appointed to take charge of the hospital (1613) in which they were to remain right up to our own days, and who with inexhaustible devotedness tended the sick notwithstanding the paucity of their resources, much yet remained to be done for this crowd of sufferers, and many reforms both in nursing and hygiene still remained to be carried out. The Ladies of Charity who visited the Hôtel-Dieu very soon noticed this and did their best to apply a remedy. But here again the need of a rule and some general direction, if individual efforts were to bear any fruit, quickly became apparent. ' Mademoiselle Le Gras and some other devout ladies, having observed in their visits to those poor patients that there was great need for many alleviations of their lot, which the Hôtel-Dieu could not supply, communicated this fact to M. Vincent.' It was Madame Goussault, with her customary energy and spirit of initiative, who led this new campaign, and ended by obtaining the consent of Saint Vincent, who was as ever prudent and slow to take up fresh undertakings. ' She often went,' Abelly continues, ' to visit the sick in the Hôtel-Dieu, and not finding things there as orderly as she would have desired, and indeed as they have since become, she had recourse to M. Vincent, begging him to extend his charity to those poor people and to reflect on the ways and means of procuring some help for this great hospital. But as he always acted in every matter with prudence and discretion, he did not at first think he should, as he said, put his sickle into another's harvest, or intrude for any purpose into a hospital which had for its administrators and directors, both in spiritual and in temporal matters, persons whom he regarded as very wise and very capable of making any regulations that might be required.'

The hospital, as a matter of fact, depended on the Canons of Notre-Dame, and as we have just said, was administered by a Congregation of Augustinian Nuns which had been expressly created to take charge, and which had its novitiate in the hospital itself. This explains S. Vincent de Paul's reluctance to make any move. But 'the President,' who could not easily be discouraged about anything which she regarded as a good enterprise, did not hesitate to call upon the Archbishop of Paris, Mgr de Gondi, and to give expression to her views and wishes. The latter, whilst warmly praising S. Vincent's reserve, easily allowed himself to be persuaded, and let him know, as Abelly[12] again tells us, 'that he would be very pleased if M. Vincent accepted the suggestion to establish an association of ladies who would give some special care to the sick of the Hôtel-Dieu, and if he gave some thought to forming such an association.' S. Vincent, confronted with a formal invitation, which he may perhaps have secretly desired, could do nothing but submit.

He authorised Madame Goussault to call a meeting of the Ladies of Charity to consult as to the means of carrying out the project, and declared that he was prepared to preside over it. This first meeting took place in July 1634, in Madame Goussault's town house in the Rue Roi-de-Sicile. As Mademoiselle Le Gras, who had been sent by S. Vincent to visit the ' charities ' at Grigny, near Corbeil, and the surrounding districts, could not be present, he wrote to her immediately. ' The grace of our Lord be ever with you.[13] The meeting took place yesterday at Madame Goussault's. Mesdames de Villesavin, de Bailleul, du Mercq, de Sainctot, and Pollalion were present. The proposal to form an association to visit the Hôtel-Dieu was agreed on, and it was decided to hold another meeting next Monday; furthermore, that in the meantime the whole affair should be commended to God and they should go to Holy Communion with that intention. Each member should also lay the matter before the ladies and young girls of her own acquaintance. . . . You and your daughters will be badly needed. It is thought that four will be wanted. Hence the necessity for taking thought to supply suitable Sisters. . . . Well, now you see how the object of your labours is growing. So get as strong as you possibly can. . . . I praise and bless God a thousand times for restoring you to health, and I beseech Him to preserve it and to bring you back in safety. . . . So return then about the end of this week,[14] or even sooner.' He wrote again : ' If an opportunity arises, come back not by water but in a good, strong cart : Mademoiselle Dufay tells me she was not able to procure a carriage.' The second meeting took place a few days later and Mademoiselle Le Gras was now able to attend. Amongst the ten ladies present will be found, in addition to those already mentioned by S. Vincent in his letter, Madame Séguier, the Chancellor's wife, Madame de Traversay, and the ' kind and holy ' Madame Fouquet.

The principle on which the undertaking was to

be carried out having been adopted at the first
meeting, the next step was how to organise it.
Madame Goussault, whilst retaining at her own
special request the title she bore at the conference
of the Ladies of Charity, namely, that of ' Sister
Servant of Charity,' was elected president, or
' superior ' to use the title then employed. ' Good
Mademoiselle Viole ' who cheered and edified
S. Vincent so greatly, was appointed assistant, and
Madame Pollalion, secretary. S. Vincent, as was
fitting and in accordance with the express wish of
the Archbishop of Paris, was nominated spiritual
director of the association. His first historian
reports in a style of great simplicity, which, though
at times affected, is not without a charm of its own,
the address given by the director of this new association to the ladies who had taken up the work with
such good will. He explained how they were to set
about the work and what was expected of them.
A few extracts from this type of familiar instruction
in which one may discern the profoundly original
and personal note of the saint and of the orator will
enable the reader to recognise its quality far better
than anything we could say.

Having first pointed out the merit and importance
of the enterprise, he warned them, says Abelly[15]
' that it would not be without opposition on the part
of some persons who might be hostile to it, as they
believed that these charitable actions might bring to
light certain failings of the hospital at this time ;
hence they should be persuaded that if much good
might be done, there were also many difficulties
to be overcome, and that it was necessary to prepare

themselves for them and to adopt suitable measures ; hereupon he did not fail to give them the most suitable advice as to how they should act. For his own part, he believed he should first of all inform both the spiritual and temporal administrators of this hospital, acquainting them with the good intentions of those devout and charitable ladies and of the command given by the Archbishop so that they might be willing to accept the aid they proposed to render the sick, as indeed they did.

' Lastly, having nominated those who were to begin this charitable visitation of the sick, poor, and others who might succeed them, he recommended them, as he had already done on several occasions : first, to invoke the help of our Lord when they entered the hospital daily, for He is the true Father of the poor, and also the intercession of the Most Holy Virgin and Saint Louis, the founder of this house ; secondly, to present themselves before the nuns who have charge of the sick, and offer to serve the latter together with the nuns so that they might share in the merits of their good works ; thirdly, to esteem and respect these nuns as visible angels, addressing and treating them with the utmost respect ; fourthly, if it should happen that these good persons did not always accept their advances in good part, they should excuse them and endeavour to see their point of view and how they felt, never contradicting or grieving or trying to get the better of them. . . . We propose, he said to them again, to contribute to the salvation and comfort of the poor, and this cannot be done without the help and good will of those nuns who are in charge. It is

only just therefore to honour them as if they were
your mothers and to treat them as spouses of the
Holy Spirit and the ladies of the house ; for it is
the mark of the spirit of God to act graciously and
the most certain means of succeeding is to love the
spirit of God by acting in this way.' Thus guided,
the Ladies, and the Daughters of Charity who were
their assistants, had no difficulty in carrying out
their appointed task and soon saw their services
appreciated as they should be.

Having observed the insufficient supply of food
given to the patients, who received nothing but the
barest necessaries of life and who were unable to
procure 'any little delicacy,' they hired, at the
suggestion of Madame Goussault, 'a room near the
Hôtel-Dieu in order to prepare and keep there
syrups, fruits, and linen . . . which were distributed from that centre to the sick. It was also
resolved to employ the Daughters of Charity in
buying and preparing all that was necessary and in
helping the Ladies to distribute the light repasts
intended for the sick.' 'The Ladies,' Abelly goes
on to say, 'went as a rule to the Hôtel-Dieu at one
o'clock in the afternoon and remained there until
four. After a visit to the Blessed Sacrament, they
put on white aprons and then in groups of four
visited each of the wards, passing from bed to bed
to offer the patients soup, milk, white bread, biscuits,
preserves, sugar-plums or fruits, cherries, grapes,
according to the season.

'If any patient was so weak as not to be able to
take the food himself, they fed him, having first
said grace. . . . The Daughters of Charity followed

the Ladies bearing plates and dishes and helping
the latter to distribute the food. When they had
gone through the wards, all went and laid aside their
aprons and proceeded to the Chapel to pay a visit
of thanksgiving for the honour our Lord had just
conferred on them by accepting them to serve
Him.'

The material assistance thus given to the sick with
so much charity, was intended to serve as an opening for a few words of devout exhortation, and as an
opportunity for the Ladies to hasten the return of
those who had wandered away from God.

This part of their task was the most delicate, and
Mademoiselle Le Gras realised it immediately.
S. Vincent, at her request, even drew up a set of
instructions which were intended to indicate the
best method to be followed so that nothing should
be wanting in prudence and charity, whilst at the
same time nothing necessary should be neglected.
' It is true,' he wrote to Louise de Marillac,[16] ' that
it is expedient to see the ladies again, both to give
them some advice on this subject as well as to teach
them how they should instruct the sick in making
their examination of conscience and in discovering
their sins.' And the saint, fully informed by
Mademoiselle Le Gras, gave a series of instructions
on this matter, replete with his habitual simplicity
as well as that penetrating and subtle discrimination which is so characteristic of him. He even
suggested to them, not without a touch of sly
humour, to dress as simply as possible so as not to
hurt the feelings of these poor sick people, ' who,
seeing the extravagances and superfluities of the

rich, are as a rule all the more grieved as they themselves have not even the necessaries of life.'

He then recommended them not to play the blue-stocking, always to hold in their hands a little book containing the principal truths of the Christian religion, which was published for this purpose, never to draw attention to, but always to efface themselves in their exhortations behind expressions such as ' This is what I have been taught. . . . This is what has been suggested to me. . . . This is the way I have been taught how to go to confession and how to pray.' Louise de Marillac, whom S. Vincent had selected to be a member of the company of the Hôtel-Dieu, and whose Daughters assisted the ladies and made up for the latters' inexperience, devoted herself from the beginning of this work which suited her so admirably ; she did so with so much zeal that her director had to moderate it. ' As for the Hôtel-Dieu,' he writes,[17] 'it is not expedient for you to be there always and it would be better if you just visited it from time to time. Do not be afraid of undertaking anything you can do without visiting it too often ; only be afraid of the idea of doing more than what you actually do, and that God may not give you the means of accomplishing it, and give yourself to His divine Majesty with the intention of never doing more than what you now do. The contrary idea makes me tremble with fear, because it seems a crime for those who are the children of God's Providence ; I praise His divine Goodness because yesterday you relieved me of such a fear.' Mademoiselle Le Gras in fact carried out this duty of visiting the sick with her accustomed charity and zeal and with that true simplicity which gives so much power to those who possess it because nothing is ever as efficacious as the truth. ' My heart,' she wrote in a note that sums up her thoughts and resolutions on this subject, ' must endeavour to elicit the same affections in myself as those I desire to expend on them, so that I may speak to them lovingly and not *at all as if I were performing a duty.*' One may easily understand then that guided by such masters as S. Vincent de Paul and her who called herself ' his little daughter and servant,' the work of the Ladies of Charity, aided and sustained by the first Daughters of Charity, made such rapid progress, produced such great results and, to employ Abelly's expressions once more, ' brought forth fruits of benediction. In the first year, not to speak of subsequent ones, the blessing of God was so abundant that more than seven hundred and sixty persons who had strayed from the true faith, including Lutherans, Calvinists, and even Turks, several of whom had been wounded and captured at sea, were converted and embraced the true religion.'

This great charitable undertaking, promoted by S. Vincent de Paul in the middle of the seventeenth century, would deserve a much more detailed study than we can here afford to give it. Mademoiselle Le Gras took a very great share in it both by her unwearying devotedness, the clarity and certainty of her mind and judgement and by her training of the Daughters of Charity, for the latter always remained her first and dearest work, serving as it did as a foundation for the energies of the Ladies of Charity.

Hence, notwithstanding her visits to the hospitals, her incessant journeys to the districts around Paris to make a visitation of and to establish ' charities,' which were multiplying in all directions, the care of ' her dear Daughters ' ever remained her primary occupation and the one which, as the future was to reveal so clearly, was to prove the most fruitful and most truly Christian. In her letters to Saint Vincent, she constantly returns to this point, pre-occupied as she was not only with the general development and extension of a work, from which some ' glory,' as men were then accustomed to say, might accrue, but much more with the formation of each and every one of her subjects, for she strove to make each a true Sister of Charity, worthy of the name of ' servant of the poor.' Saint Vincent was no less in earnest about this matter, and nothing is more touching than to see with what care, what Christian solicitude, and also with what gracious firmness and lucidity of judgement they laboured together at the training of the first Sisters of Charity. They were at one in never preferring numbers or external gifts and qualities to the ' things of the spirit,' to the acquisition of virtues or the firm will to acquire them, in a word, to holiness of life, to employ the term in its largest and widest sense, which nothing can replace. ' I shall see your daughters,'[18] Saint Vincent wrote to her at the end of one of his letters, ' both together and separately, and you will tell me whatever you please as soon as possible.' Moreover, in almost every letter remarks will be found about this or that ' dear daughter,' which show the persevering attention he devoted

to each individual, and also ' Mademoiselle's ' care
to inform him on every subject so that she might
have his ideas and guidance. Such care and
attention, such solicitude on the part of these great
souls, who were so profoundly and perfectly
Christian in every sense of the word, could not and
as a matter of fact did not remain sterile. Mademoiselle Le Gras' little company, which as we shall see
in a moment was to become officially that of ' the
Daughters of Charity and Servants of the Poor,'
rapidly increased and its members were not slow to
walk in the footsteps of their teachers. Hence,
wherever they were known, even from the moment
they had begun to carry out their mission, the
people demanded their presence. This was a result
utterly unexpected by Louise de Marillac's humility,
but she accommodated herself to it with the perfect
simplicity of really humble souls to whom the idea
never even occurs of attributing to themselves any
share in an enterprise, the success of which they
refer to God's grace and goodness. As the number
of Sisters had increased and was daily increasing, it
became necessary to look for new quarters. The
first house in the Rue des Fossés-Saint-Victor, now
Rue Cardinal Lemoine, had become much too con-
fined. After much seeking, a house situated at
Chapelle Saint-Denys, then a village close to the
Faubourg of that name, was decided on. The
building was much larger, and above all, it had the
great advantage of being close to the Priory of
Saint-Lazare, to which Vincent de Paul had just
brought the members of his new Congregation and
from which the name ' Lazarists ' has come to be

applied to them.   On the one hand, this was a
complete change of residence which meant living
almost in the country, but on the other, it provided,
together with more space and air, the calm and
solitude always requisite for novitiates, and for
those of the active life especially.   In the month of
May 1636, Louise de Marillac arrived at La Chapelle
with her little band of Daughters.   She immediately resumed her usual life of work and prayer,
whilst she laboured to train and form others who
would imitate and rival her example.   The small
house in the Rue Saint-Victor was still used by a few
Sisters who were employed in looking after the
' Charity ' established in that parish.

NOTES ON CHAPTER III

[1] *Conferences of S. Vincent de Paul to the Daughters of
Charity*, 1902 edition, p. 6.

[2] *Op. cit.*, Conf. I, p. 1.

[3] *Letters of S. Vincent de Paul*, L. CIV, p. 141.

[4] *Letters of S. Vincent de Paul to Louise de Marillac*, No.
LXXIII, p. 100.

[5] *Conferences of S. Vincent de Paul*, Conf. I, p. 3.

[6] *Op. cit.*, p. 3.

[7] *Op. cit.*, p. 5.

[8] *Op. cit.*, Conf. VII, p. 23.

[9] *Letters of S. Vincent de Paul*, No. CII, p. 136.

[10] *Op. cit.*, p. 137.

[11] Abelly, *Life of S. Vincent de Paul*, Bk. I, p. 174.

[12] *Op. cit.*, Bk. I, p. 174.

[13] *Letters of S. Vincent de Paul*, No. LXXV, p. 102.

[14] *Op. cit.*, No. LXXVII, p. 105.

[15] Abelly, *op. cit.*, Bk. I, p. 176.

[16] *Letters of S. Vincent de Paul*, No. LXXVII, p. 105.

[17] *Op. cit.*, No. LXXXI, p. 110.

[18] *Op. cit.*, No. LXXXI, p. 110.

CHAPTER IV

RETREATS—PRIMARY   SCHOOLS—FOUNDLINGS—THE
HOSPITAL AT ANGERS—THE GALLEY SLAVES
1636–1640

WHEN Louise de Marillac left the little home which had formed the cradle, as it were, of her undertaking, she did not do so without regret or an interior struggle. If indeed she had been brought into closer proximity with S. Vincent de Paul she was now at a greater distance from her son, who was completing his studies on the Hill of S. Geneviève, and who continued to occupy her thoughts to such an extent as to cause her at times much care and anxiety. But whenever she saw the Will of God clearly indicated, it was enough to make her strive for its fulfilment, without a murmur or a deliberate thought of self or her own convenience. Hence Mademoiselle Le Gras wrote at this period in a note-book of hers still in existence, the following observations which are characterised by a true and penetrating simplicity and are redolent of entire self-abandonment and complete forgetfulness of self, on what she judged, with her strong good sense, to be the Will of God in her regard, and on her duty to help forward the extension of His Kingdom.

' Hence, no more self-will, and may Thy will alone
reign in me ; grant me this grace, O my Jesus !
by the love Thou dost bear me and by the intercession of Thy Holy Mother who so perfectly loved
all that flows from Thy most amiable Will. I implore
this grace with all my heart and abandon myself
entirely to Thee, beseeching Thy goodness not to
look upon the contrary dispositions that are in me,
and desiring that the power of Thy love may compel,
by the sweetness of its strength, the consent of all
my senses that might be opposed to it. I will go to
my new home with the intention of honouring Divine
Providence which leads me there, and I will dispose
myself to do there all that this same Providence may
allow to be effected. By this change of dwelling-
place, I shall honour that of Jesus and His Holy
Mother when they went from Bethlehem to Egypt
and subsequently to other places and I shall not
desire, any more than they did, to have a dwelling-
place of my own in this world.'[1]

The house at Chapelle Saint-Denys, which was
then almost in the country, was not to be for Louise
de Marillac a place of repose for the few years she
resided there with her Daughters ; far from it, for
it was in this new home, as we shall explain in a
moment, that she began several of her greatest
works. But what she sought was neither rest nor a
period of repose, but work for the welfare of souls
and for the relief of the poor. Yet she never lost
sight of her own spiritual perfection, which, like a
true daughter of S. Vincent de Paul, she well knew
provided the indispensable basis of any really good
and profitable external activity. She also knew,

and every day brought it home to her more clearly, the originality of her special type of religious devotedness ; that is to say, the two forms of life—the inner and the outer—instead of interfering with or injuring each other, were mutually helpful and necessary. The life of prayer, far from hindering, helped the active life, and if the latter could not exist without prayer and meditation, prayer and the inner life, in their turn, might derive great profit from external works carried out with a true love for God and her neighbour, so that, to use a well-worn and oft repeated comparison, they served the faithful soul as two wings by which it might raise itself up to God. The union of these two forms of life hitherto distinct, at least in the case of women, is the most original feature of the work undertaken by Louise de Marillac. It is her characteristic note, to use a modern formula.

She was foremost in giving an example to her Daughters, for she taught them to devote themselves wholeheartedly to the poor and the sick, and some time later, to the education and instruction of young children, without ever allowing these occupations to prevent them from living in the presence of God, for whose sake all their actions were accomplished. She also taught them to *take their cloister about with them* always and everywhere and never to leave it, whether in the midst of the noise and bustle of great cities or in the silence of the fields or peaceful villages. This was a great novelty and one that went directly against all the prevalent ideas of that time. There was an element almost of rashness about it, which we can scarcely conceive to-day, but

H

which is clearly revealed in the celebrated words of
Saint Vincent which were subsequently placed at
the beginning of the rules of the little Company :
' The Daughters of Charity shall have for their only
monastery the homes of the sick, for a chapel their
parish church, for their cloister the streets of the city
or the wards of a hospital, for a grille the fear of
God, and for a veil holy modesty.'[2]

These, certainly, were very new ideas. We shall
now see how and to what extent Louise de Marillac
succeeded in carrying them out.

The years she spent at La Chapelle were not, as we
have remarked, years of solitude or repose ; quite
the contrary, they represent a particularly active and
fruitful period in her life. It was, in fact, the time
in which retreats for persons living in the world,
the teaching of Catechism and the opening of
schools for little girls, and the commencement of
the work on behalf of foundlings and galley-
slaves, had their first beginnings ; and it was also
from La Chapelle that she started out to instal her
Daughters in the first hospital placed entirely under
their control—the hospital of Angers. And all this
was carried on without any cessation from the
establishment of ' charities '—quite the contrary—
and without neglecting for a moment or devoting
less attention to the spiritual training and formation
of her Daughters, whose numbers kept on increasing. We have not sufficient space here at our
disposal to give any detailed account of the various
undertakings which were destined to play such a
great part in the religious and charitable life of
France as well as in other countries. We shall just

briefly indicate them, but the mere enumeration is of itself enough to help us to form a sound judgement on the ardent zeal which, under a calm and serene exterior, burned up this wonderful spirit ever inflamed with that mysterious fire which Jesus Christ came on earth to enkindle.

Not indeed that Louise de Marillac voluntarily sought out and spent her energies on new forms of good works. Far from it, but docile in this as in all else to the lessons of her spiritual guide and following his example, she let the Divine Will clearly manifest to her whatever work was to be undertaken. Never did she take the initiative, yet never did she refuse to take up a task allotted to her. In this way, she put into practice, perhaps unconsciously, that well-known maxim which has guided so many saints : to ask nothing and to refuse nothing. Thus, shortly after her arrival at La Chapelle, she made a retreat from which she gathered great spiritual fruit. She mentioned the fact to Madame Goussault who asked if she might do the same in Louise's own home. Mademoiselle Le Gras, far from refusing, joyfully consented ; she soon perceived the value and consolation her friend had procured from this exercise and saw in it an indication of the value of such retreats, even for persons living in the world. Profiting by the room at her disposal in her new home, she suggested the idea to several ladies of her acquaintance who expressed a wish to follow Madame Goussault's example. The suggestion was entertained and followed at first by a few, and then by a much larger number of ladies of the highest rank who imitated Madame

Goussault's example. In this way, the making of 'closed' retreats by persons living in the world was first established. It was destined to continue despite changing social conditions, to spread in a thousand different forms, and to produce from the beginning as abundant fruits as it does in our own days wherever it is still carried on.

So, too, it was during her sojourn at La Chapelle that Louise de Marillac began to apply her Daughters to the instruction of little girls and to the teaching of catechism. Hitherto, they had only visited the poor and nursed the sick as helpers and substitutes for the Ladies of Charity. It was now for the first time that they opened a school. But as the new school might possibly injure the one that was already in existence at La Chapelle, Louise de Marillac offered the man in charge a sum of money as a compensation. She did not wish, she said, that any one could say she had injured a single individual by bringing the Daughters of Charity to La Chapelle. This modest beginning of the Sisters in the work of 'the little schools' as the term then went, was the object of her special care and attention, and as it was destined subsequently to produce much admirable fruit it should not be passed over without calling some attention to it. The little grain of seed, sown by Saint Vincent's fellow-worker and daughter, was destined to produce that marvellous harvest which men have ever since admired. At the present day, when the 'dear Sisters' are being driven out of the primary schools all over France, we are in even a better position to judge the value and importance of Louise de Marillac's attempt, during her sojourn in the village of La Chapelle Saint-Denys, despite the other heavy and numerous tasks to which she had put her hand. It should not be forgotten that this work on behalf of education was effected in the midst of the anxieties and agitations produced by the Thirty Years' War, the effects of which were felt in Paris and its environs.

It was, as a matter of fact, in the July of this year 1636, shortly after Louise had taken up her residence in her new home, that the terrible John de Werth, at the head of an army of Spaniards whose numbers were increased by bands of Hungarians and pillagers of every nationality, broke through the northern frontiers, plundered Picardy and pushed on squadrons of cavalry that spread terror in all directions. The River Oise was crossed and some horsemen even got as far as Compiègne a few days after the siege of Corbie was begun. We can imagine the terror of the country people flying before the enemy and seeking refuge in Paris and the country round about the capital, in their belief that here at least they would be in safety.

The panic was intense even in Paris, from which many of the inhabitants had begun to fly, carrying away with them their most cherished possessions. 'Paris,'[3] wrote Saint Vincent, 'is expecting to be besieged by the Spaniards, who have entered Picardy and are ravaging it with a powerful army whose advance-guard is only ten or twelve leagues off, so that the people from the neighbouring districts have fled to Paris, and the city itself is in such a fright that many of its inhabitants are flying to other cities. The King, however, is endeavouring to

muster up an army to oppose it, as his own troops
are absent or at the extremities of the Kingdom,
and the place where they are mustering and arming
the battalions is this very house. The stables, the
wood-sheds, the halls and cloisters are piled with
arms and the court-yards with soldiers. Even
to-day, the Feast of the Assumption, is not
free from all this noise and tumult. The drums
began to beat even before seven o'clock in the
morning, so that since eight o'clock seventy-two
companies have been mustered here.'

The house in which Louise de Marillac and her
Daughters had taken up their residence was quite
close to Saint-Lazare, of which Saint Vincent is
speaking, and was thus right in the midst of all the
tumult produced by the fears of a siege, and the
crowds of terrified peasants who had fled before the
invasion. Mademoiselle Le Gras and her little flock
never even thought of flying, but on the contrary,
profited by the ordeal to practise once again those
works of charity to which they had dedicated their
lives. Her house at La Chapelle was thrown open
to such poor girls and women as could find no
shelter. As long as the fear of an invasion lasted,
it was transformed into a refuge. 'It was here,'
says her first biographer,[4] ' that she began to exercise
the virtue of hospitality. A large number of girls
from the frontiers of Picardy having been forced to
abandon their homes out of fear of the enemy
which had entered this province and was besieging
the town of Corbie, found in her community an
asylum both for their lives and their virtue. And
in order to practise hospitality in its highest per-

fection, she not only supplied them with board and lodging, but added to this spiritual refreshment by a retreat which she arranged for them.' Notwithstanding these unexpected anxieties and troubles, Louise de Marillac did not relax for a moment her solicitude for her Daughters and the ' charities ' which she still kept on founding. But her health, always frail, suffered severely from all this overwork ; to such an extent, indeed, that Vincent de Paul for a moment even advised her to leave Paris, but she paid no heed to this suggestion. The retirement of the Spaniards and the raising of the siege of Corbie at length allowed her to resume her ordinary occupations which were in fact increasing day by day. The rescue of abandoned children, ' The Foundlings,' a work which has most popularised the name of S. Vincent de Paul and which has even given rise to a legend, was also undertaken during those same years. Here also Louise de Marillac was by his side, helping and sustaining him by her zeal and enlightened intelligence in all that concerns the welfare of the poor. For it was a marked feature in the character of the very original woman with whom we are concerned that the practice of the widest and most active charity was united with a judgement as solid as it was practical, which saw things as they are, without prejudice or illusion, and which sought to remedy evils as far as possible without ever desiring to accomplish impossibilities, but yet without ever losing hope in the power of Divine Grace which can face and overcome all obstacles. We need not give a detailed account here of this work for the

Foundlings, which has been so often related and which has been popularised by the art of the painter and engraver. All we are now concerned with is the part played herein by Louise de Marillac, and this was, as ever, discreet and hidden, yet active, and we may even say preponderant. She had already on several occasions, as may be gathered from a letter of Saint Vincent's, called his attention to the wretched state of the foundlings who were gathered together in a house known as ' La Couche ' where they lacked the most elementary attention and were made the victims of the most abominable traffic. But it was only towards the end of the year 1635 that Saint Vincent, slow as ever to make a move, made up his mind to speak on the subject to the Ladies of Charity, and to suggest to them a new form of doing good. This, at least, is the conclusion to be arrived at from reading his letters and the accounts given us by his first biographers. At Saint Vincent's suggestion, the Ladies of Charity of the Hôtel-Dieu paid a visit to ' La Couche ' and were so shocked by the dreadful spectacle that met their eyes that they resolved to make some attempt to better the lot of these unfortunate abandoned children, no matter what difficulties they might have to contend with. On January 1, 1636, Vincent de Paul wrote to Louise de Marillac :[5] ' Mademoiselle . . . it was decided at the last meeting that you should be asked to try and do something about the foundlings, and to see if there is any means of providing them with cows' milk and of removing two or three of the children. I felt consoled that Providence was turning to you to do this. I know quite well there are many things to be discussed about this matter, and we shall speak of them on another occasion. . . . Madame Goussault does not seem to me to be very well. Take care of your own health. I wish you a new heart and a completely new love for Him who loves us unceasingly and as tenderly as if He were just beginning to love us, for all God's love of us is ever new and full of variety though He never changes.' Louise de Marillac had not to be asked twice and she began at once to collect foundling children and to strive to rear them both physically and morally as well as she could.

The beginnings of this new work were of a very modest nature and then, in 1636, after another address by Vincent de Paul to the Ladies of Charity, ' they resolved,'[6] says the first biographer of Louise, ' to commence by receiving twelve children, and as the number was too great for the Ladies to take charge of them all, the children were to be chosen by lot ; this number was to be increased from time to time, in accordance with their ability to do so, and it was not without great regret that they saw themselves unable to receive them all.'

The attempt was begun at La Chapelle, under Louise de Marillac's guidance, but the house was unsuited to this form of work and already contained the Daughters of Charity who were being trained under their mother's eye. Hence it became necessary to look out for a site for this new charitable undertaking. A house was hired in the Rue des Boulangers, in the Faubourg Saint-Victor, between the Rue des Fossés-Saint-Victor and the Rue

Saint-Victor, and the 'Foundlings' were installed there. 'Here is a new task for you,' wrote Saint Vincent to Louise,[7] 'I mean the transferring of the little foundlings and the order to be observed in their new home. I beg you, Mademoiselle, to set to work at it to-morrow and to send me an account of what you may have done on Saturday.' A lady named Pelletier was placed in charge of this new establishment, but under the control of Louise de Marillac to whom she was to give an account from time to time of how matters were progressing, 'as, for instance, every week or at least every fortnight.' Louise de Marillac even went and stayed there for a week to set things going. 'We have considered your statement,' Saint Vincent wrote to her,[8] 'at two meetings of the officers of the Charity of the Hôtel-Dieu, and, on Sunday next, we shall communicate the decision, in the form of a code of rules, to Madame Pelletier, to see if she is willing to fall in with them. Madame Goussault, in the presence of the officers, will do this. The whole assembly considers it essential that this house should be subject to the Superioress of the Daughters of Charity, as I have already written to you, and that you should spend seven or eight days there, if your health permits.'

Finally, in 1640, after a meeting at which Saint Vincent spoke and put before them the miserable state of those poor little creatures forsaken from their birth, when the Ladies of Charity decided to take over the work of the Foundlings as a whole, the question arose of accepting every child that might be offered. Here again it was to Louise de

Marillac that the Ladies of Charity turned for the organisation of this further extension of the work which seemed almost beyond their powers, ' seeing,' as Abelly remarks,[9], ' that at this period they had only an assured income of twelve or fourteen hundred *livres.*'   As the house in the Rue Saint-Victor had now become too small, it was necessary to send the children out to nurse in the country, in the environs of Paris, and occasionally to places much more distant.   Almost all the work of organisation fell on Louise, and she devoted herself to it with her customary zeal, supervising every detail and arranging for the admission of the children, for having them visited to see that they were not neglected, and also to see that they were baptised. In fact, she showed herself a ' real mother ' to the children, who had been cast aside by those who had brought them into the world.   But if her courage and ardour were fully up to the standard of the task that had been allotted to her by God, her bodily strength grew gradually less and frequently failed her.   Hence she was forced to take many precautions and to nurse herself, as the phrase goes, and this grieved her deeply, so much as to make her long for that other life where there will be no such necessity.   One day she asked Saint Vincent if it were not time for her to die.   ' I am pained,' he replied,[10] ' at what you ask me.   Oh !   It is not time, Mademoiselle ;   you are too much needed in this world.   In the name of God, do all that is possible for your health, and treat yourself more kindly.'

Louise de Marillac was not one of those persons

who are easily attacked and paralysed by discouragement; far from it; from these brief periods in which the pressure of earthly cares had caused her to long for the joys of Heaven, she came forth more ardent, more active, more fully and joyously devoted than ever. Hence, scarcely had she recovered from the grief and shock of the death of her beloved friend, Madame Goussault, who had so loyally aided and sustained her in all her enterprises, than she set out, in the month of November 1639, to establish her Daughters in Angers, where they had been asked to take charge of a hospital. Although she was still an invalid and had been warned that the plague was raging in that city and its environs, nothing could turn her aside from undertaking a journey which must have been most fatiguing.

Louise de Marillac arrived in Angers with some of her most experienced Daughters towards the end of November 1639, having travelled by coach as far as Orleans and then by water on the river Loire for the remainder and the longer part of the journey. This foundation at Angers marks a date in the life of Mademoiselle Le Gras, and is of sufficient importance for us to dwell upon it for a moment.

It was the first occasion that the Daughters of Charity were officially placed, so to say, in charge of a hospital. Hitherto, they had only been called in to render temporary assistance as helpers and to co-operate with the Ladies of Charity. But, on this occasion, at the request of the governors of the hospital, the ' Masters ' or ' Fathers of the poor,' as they were called, were to take sole charge of the management of the city hospital at Angers. Now this hospital was excessively badly managed, from every point of view : the treatment of the sick, from both the physical and moral standpoint, was very far from being what it should. Accordingly, it was essential to effect an entire reformation and at the same time to carry out a very difficult task. The Sisters were to pass from a secondary or at least a subordinate rôle to the front place, and in short to assume a heavy responsibility. We may therefore understand why Louise de Marillac wished to be present at the installation of her Daughters and to instruct them fully in all the duties they would now be asked to carry out.

After travelling for a fortnight, Louise and her companions arrived at Angers where they were received by the Abbé de Vaux, the Vicar General of the diocese, who had taken a prominent part in the negotiations for their coming. The long journey over wretched roads or in a canal boat exposed to all the winds of Heaven had exhausted the strength of the leader of the little band, and Louise at once fell so gravely ill that Saint Vincent de Paul wrote to her :[11] ' So there you are, Mademoiselle, ill by the order of Providence. May His holy name be blessed ! I hope from His loving kindness that He will again be glorified by this illness as He has been by all the others, and that is what I pray for unceasingly, both here and elsewhere wherever I go. Ah ! how I should wish our Lord to let you see how heartily everyone is praying to Him, and the tender affection of all the officers of the " Charity " of the Hôtel-Dieu, when I spoke to them the day before yesterday at a little meeting. I implore you, Mademoiselle, to do all that you possibly can to recover your health and to spare yourself nothing, above all if you are in need of money. The Abbé de Vaux will not refuse to advance some until I can send it to you, which I will do if you let me know. As for your return, you must come back in a litter ; we shall try to send you one when you are able to travel.' Nevertheless, Louise de Marillac, aided perhaps by her energetic will, recovered, and as soon as ever she felt better, she moved with her Daughters into the hospital which they were to serve and which they found in a state of complete disorder. The patients were utterly neglected, and dirt and carelessness reigned all over the place. 'There were,' says a brief account drawn up by one of the Saint's companions, 'thirty or forty patients men and women, and only three dozen under garments in all. . . . It was pitiful to see so much disorder and so much waste of what belonged to the poor.' The need of a thorough reformation made itself felt in every department. Hence, after some hesitation, the prudent Mother of the ' Daughters of Charity ' decided to sign an agreement with the governors of the hospital by which its maintenance and direction were entrusted to her Daughters. ' You will do so,' Saint Vincent wrote to her on the subject,[12] ' *in nomine Domini* : you may sign this agreement in your own name as *directress of the Daughters of Charity, servants of the poor sick in hospitals and parishes*, under the authority of the Superior-General of the Congregation of Priests

of the Mission and director of the said Daughters
of Charity. . . . People are praying to God for
you in many places in Paris ; everyone is interested
in the state of your health ; and you cannot imagine
to what an extent.'

This agreement, which has since served as a model
for countless others, would deserve to be given in
full as it reveals so admirably the prudence, wisdom,
and moderation that characterise all the enterprises
of Louise de Marillac, the docile follower of her
spiritual father in this as in so many other higher
paths.   However, we shall only give the following
passage in which the rights and duties of the parties
are delimited with perfect equity.[13] ' The Daughters
of Charity shall always abide under the government
of the Superior-General of the Mission, and no one
shall hinder them from living according to their
rule, which, indeed, obliges them to leave everything whenever the service of the poor demands it.
In all that concerns temporal matters, they shall be
entirely subject to the administrators and shall obey
them exactly.   But they, and they alone, shall have
charge of the poor and no others may be associated
with them in this work. . . . They shall be boarded
and maintained, both in health and in sickness, at
the expense of the hospital, and shall be treated in
every respect as daughters of the house and not as
hirelings.   They shall not be obliged to nurse the
sick outside the wards of the hospital.   They shall
render an account of their service only to the administrators, and the latter should bear in mind that if
they do not support the Sisters in their dealings
either with servants or the poor, the Sisters cannot

effect any good, hence they should support the Sisters by their authority, and never publicly reprimand them for their failings, but shall point them out in private, and the Sisters will, aided by God's grace, correct their mistakes. . . .

' . . . In case a Sister should die, the administrators, remembering that she was consecrated to the service of God and of the poor, shall permit her companions to bury her in a becoming manner and in accordance with their usual practice. . . . The Superior-General in Paris may change the Sisters whenever he deem it advisable to do so. The administrators, on their side, may demand, at the expense of the hospital, the removal of such Sisters as may not have given satisfaction, after having tried them, however, for a year or two, and after giving the Superior-General timely notice.'

Meanwhile, the Daughters (as they were called) received from Louise de Marillac a special set of rules which prescribed the method of nursing the sick and the special regulations they were to observe in order that they might remain faithful to the ' rules and exercises of the little company, remembering,' as the rule went on to say, ' that the service rendered to the sick is constant prayer in the sight of God.'

The agreement was signed on February 1, 1640, and the Sisters immediately began to exercise their functions. At first five and then eight Daughters of Charity, under the direction of Louise de Marillac, set themselves courageously to work, braving all sorts of opposition in addition to the plague which was then raging in the hospital. It is Saint Vincent himself who, not without emotion, mentions this fact in one of his conferences : ' I am speaking,' he said, ' of our dear Sisters in Angers, who took charge of the hospital in that city when it was infected with contagion, and who have nursed persons attacked by the plague as readily as those who had other diseases. It seemed as if the plague respected them.'[14]   In a short space of time, their zeal and devotedness overcame every obstacle, and the hospital at Angers became a model for all others of the period.

' Since those days,'[15] a Sister afterwards wrote, ' the number of patients has increased, the wards have been well aired and the number of beds settled in the present proportion, that is to say, a hundred and ten for men, and ninety for women, without counting those who have to be treated when the necessity arises.'

Louise de Marillac was recalled to Paris by Vincent de Paul who was in need of her assistance, and she left Angers immediately after the Sisters had been installed. ' As for your return,' Saint Vincent wrote to her, ' I beg you let it be as soon as possible, and make use of a litter, hiring two good, strong horses for that purpose. I beseech you, Mademoiselle, to stint yourself in nothing, and, no matter what it costs, to procure whatever will be most convenient for you.'

Louise de Marillac set out for Paris on February 25, 1640, and, submissive to the advice of Saint Vincent, returned by the Orléans mail-coach, travelling as far as Tours in the carriage of

I

her host, the Abbé de Vaux, and from thence to Orléans in a hired covered car.

If she was recalled to Paris, it was not to take a rest there ;—quite the contrary ; for all the works which she had begun were now in need of her presence. Immediately on her arrival, she set to work once more with renewed courage, spending herself unsparingly on the formation of the Daughters of Charity, on the confraternities of charity, which were multiplying all around Paris and were even beginning to spread to distant provinces, and lastly, on the Foundlings. Furthermore, it was during these crowded and fruitful years that she undertook the care of the galley-slaves, that is to say, she consented to set apart some of her Daughters to nurse and tend men condemned to penal servitude for life, whom the Sisters also endeavoured to convert. S. Vincent de Paul had for many years past devoted himself to the service of these wretched men ; he had first of all succeeded in having some of them transferred from the depôt where they awaited removal to the galleys, to a house in which, though well guarded and supervised by soldiers, they could be treated with a little more humanity than in the common prison, and where their souls as well as their bodies might be attended to. In 1639, Monsieur Cornuel, a Paris banker, left a special legacy for the relief and comfort of men condemned to the galleys, and this enabled Saint Vincent to carry on the work. It was at this period that he set aside some Sisters of Charity to look after the convicts ; they were entrusted with the men's spiritual and temporal welfare whilst they remained

in a house he had rented near the Gate of Saint-
Bernard. Louise de Marillac naturally had to co-
operate in this undertaking and to give a special
training to those of her Daughters whom S. Vincent
called ' The Daughters of the Convicts,' as this was
a particularly difficult and dangerous task. But
nothing could daunt the courage of the first superioress of the Sisters, and she drew up a ' Rule
proper for daughters destined for this employment.'

This set of regulations is especially remarkable
both for the discretion and the ardent charity which
it reveals.[16] ' As the care of the galley-slaves,' it
states, ' is one of the most difficult and dangerous
entrusted to the Sisters of Charity, both on account
of the handling of money it entails and the condition of the persons to be encountered, so also it is
one of the most meritorious and pleasing to God,
when carried out becomingly, because by doing so
we practise in a high degree the spiritual and
corporal works of mercy in regard to those most
wretched in body and soul that can be imagined.
Hence, those who are called by God to this holy
exercise should on the one hand endeavour to render
themselves worthy of it by the practice of the
requisite virtues and by an exact observance of their
rules, and on the other, should encourage themselves
to have great confidence in our Lord Jesus Christ,
considering that when they are helping those poor
people they are rendering Him a service which will
be just as, or even more, pleasing to Him than if it
were shown to Himself in person, and consequently
He will not fail to bestow on them as a recompense
the graces necessary to overcome all the difficulties

that they may meet with, in addition to the precious crown He is reserving for them in heaven.' Next come regulations for feeding the convicts, to whom the Sisters themselves will carry the meal, and if the soup-pot is too heavy they will be assisted by the warders. They shall do more ; they shall attend to the cleanliness of the prisoners, and in case of necessity, their physical needs. When the Saint has to speak on this matter she shows her customary discretion in the recommendations given to the Sisters.[17] ' They shall remember,' she says, ' to renew interiorly the spirit of purity and modesty as a safeguard against the customary impudence of such persons on these occasions.'

' . . . And although they should at all times show great modesty and reserve they shall nevertheless pay particular attention to these virtues whenever they are present in the wards to render the convicts some service, seeming to ignore their bantering remarks, unless they are utterly impudent, in which case they should speak to them seriously or leave the place.

' And, though it may be difficult to prevent them from committing such unruly acts of impudence towards the Sisters even when the latter are doing them the greatest kindnesses, they shall not cease from endeavouring to prevent them, and shall do so by means of much patience and by praying to God for them at the same time, as Saint Stephen did for those who were stoning him.' And above all they shall take the greatest care not to afford even the slightest ground for complaint ; and to that end, they shall never speak harshly to the convicts or

reproach them for the annoyance they may have caused, or contend with them in order to justify themselves, in case they are falsely accused. On the contrary, they shall endeavour not to say a word without the greatest necessity, and to treat them with gentleness and compassion, seeing the pitiable state in which they are, both in soul and body, remembering withal that they have not ceased to be the members of Him who made Himself a Slave to ransom us all from the servitude of the evil one. . . ."[18]
' And, that they may the better practise all these counsels, and that the charity they exercise in prison may redound the more to the glory of God, their own perfection and the salvation of those poor afflicted men, they shall pray several times a day to call down the Holy Spirit, that He may so purify their thoughts, words, and actions (especially when tempted against purity, in case they may be) that they may be like the sun's light which passes continually over things that are dirty without ever being soiled in the slightest. And after that, let them have confidence that God will hear their prayers, as He did those of the three children in the fiery furnace, since they have undertaken this duty only from charity and obedience.'

If we bear in mind that these powerful and beautiful words fell from the pen of a woman and were addressed to poor, simple country girls going to wait on convicts, we cannot forbear yet again from admiring and blessing the spirit of charity and love which Jesus Christ enkindled and which nothing can replace and nothing extinguish.

CHAPTER V

HER INNER LIFE AND THE DEVELOPMENT OF HER
UNDERTAKINGS—1640–1644

' YOU are more tender-hearted than any mother
I have known. . . . In the name of God,
leave your son to the care of his Heavenly Father,
for He loves him more than you do ; or, at least, get
rid of your over-eagerness.'[1] It was in this fashion
that S. Vincent de Paul, on several occasions,
reproved Mademoiselle Le Gras for her exaggerated
anxiety about her son. In the midst of all the care
and attention she bestowed on those new undertakings to which we have already referred, she continued in fact to busy herself with him in such a
lovingly maternal way that its very over-anxiety
and nervousness only reveal the more the warmth
of her heart. For, like all true Saints, Louise de
Marillac always remained the same, perfectly simple
and natural even when at the highest pitch of
devotion. During all those years of constant toil
for the cause of charity she never for a day ceased
to think of her son and to watch over him and his
future with the same solicitude as she would have
shown if she had remained in the world.

The name of ' Michel ' recurs over and over
again in her letters to S. Vincent de Paul, who on

his side, though occasionally reproaching her for
excessive anxiety about the boy, was aiding her by
his advice in a task always especially difficult in the
case of a widow, namely, how to guide a son who is
beginning life and how to secure a suitable position
for him in the world. At first she would have
liked to make him a priest, and with that in mind,
she sent him to study in various ecclesiastical
establishments, as we have already remarked, and
particularly in that of Adrian Bourdoise who was
in those days remarkable in the religious world as
an educator and trainer of young priests. Subsequently, Michel was sent to school to the Jesuits.
As these different attempts did not succeed, Saint
Vincent took him into the Collège des Bons-
Enfants so that the boy might continue his studies
there. Vincent de Paul told Louise de Marillac that
he was praying to God to grant the boy ' the same
zeal and the same graces at labouring for the salvation of souls as he had granted his mother, poor and
of little account though she be '; but this attempt
was no more successful than the others. The poor
mother was dismayed. She was afraid that her own
faults and failings were being punished in her son,
and that this was ' a testimony of God's justice on
herself.' Saint Vincent at once replied to this
remark with a freedom and briskness that goes so
well with his habitual geniality :[2] ' I have never
seen such another woman as you or one who takes
certain matters so very tragically. Your son's
choice is, you say, a manifestation of God's justice
on you. You certainly did wrong to entertain such
ideas and still more to express them. I have

already begged you not to talk like that in future. In the name of God, Mademoiselle, correct it, and learn once for all that such bitter thoughts come from the evil one and that those our Lord sends are sweet and gracious ; remember too, that the faults of children are not always to be imputed to their parents, above all when the latter have done their best to instruct and give them good example, as you have, thanks be to God. Remember, too, that our Lord permits, in His admirable Providence, the hearts of good fathers and mothers to suffer agonies. . . . By God's grace you are not one of that kind, but on the contrary, you have reason for praising God.'

This is not the place to go into details about the various attempts made by Louise de Marillac and Vincent de Paul to induce Michel Le Gras to make up his wavering mind. In the end, he abandoned the idea of the priesthood, on the advice of S. Vincent de Paul, who, seeing no signs of a vocation in the young man, was the first to suggest he should give up all such ideas. As Louise de Marillac felt this intensely, he wrote to console her :[3] ' Leave him to be guided by God who is more his father than you are his mother, and who loves him more than you do. . . . He knows quite well how to call him at some other time, if such be His will, or to give him an employment suitable to his salvation. . . . I beg you to make your prayer on the wife of Zebedee and her sons, to whom our Lord said, when she was urging Him to provide for them : "You know not what you ask." ' And, in the course of another letter, he says : ' Do not grieve

any more about young Michel's happiness. . . .
Yes, you may say to me, but it is on God's account
I am worrying. If you are worrying yourself about
serving God, then it is not for God you are distress-
ing yourself.' For many a long day the motherly
love of Louise de Marillac was to be kept on
tenterhooks for this son who resembled her so little,
and it was not until twelve years later that he settled
down by making a good marriage, as we shall see
later.

If we have stressed a little the anxiety of mind and
the doubts or fears of Louise de Marillac in regard to
her son's future, we have done so because they
seemed to us to give a marvellous picture of the
interior of this simple, natural soul which was
always the same in the midst of the most ardent
and most active life of devotion. This sensibility,
these 'tendernesses' for which Saint Vincent
sometimes reproached her with a smile, never
interfered for a moment with the practice of the
great Christian virtues, and only served to deepen
and make them even still more disinterested. They
also reveal the ardour and vivacity of her soul and
the intensity of her interior life, which, far from
being lessened by the ceaseless activity which she
displayed in the practice of all forms of exterior
charity for the poor, continued, on the contrary,
to be its ever abundant source. In the case of
Louise de Marillac, as in that of all the saints, even
those who seem to be absorbed in charitable work
for others, her inner life was the burning centre in
which were stimulated the zeal and activity that led
her to spend herself unsparingly, despite the ever

growing feebleness of her health, and the conse-
quent diminution of her physical powers.

There can be no question, in these brief pages, of
going into the details of that inner life ; as a matter
of fact, by its very intensity and elevation it would
in great part escape us. Nevertheless, it is essential
for us to say a few words about it if we are to catch
a glimpse of the incessant toil of this chosen soul
during the most active and most fruitful years of
her life, and to point out the source from which she
drew so much strength and courage. Nothing can
be more touching and instructive than the sight of
the unrelenting labour that Louise de Marillac took
with herself, even when she was spending herself
most lavishly in the service of the poor, ' our
masters,' as she used to call them. This constant
need, if not of perfection, at least of the very best,
this desire for the good (which was indeed at times
a little over-eager and which her guide always
moderated with his accustomed wisdom and cordial
friendliness), shines out clearly in the brief notes and
meditations which Louise de Marillac bequeathed
to her Daughters. These papers are the merest
sketches and yet they are fully worthy of the pious
care with which they have been preserved. An
ardent love of our Lord Jesus Christ, a desire to be
united with Him in all His states, and to attain this
union by interior perfection as well as by the
exterior works that are, as it were, its natural fruit,
a need to devote herself to prove her love and of an
utter self-annihilation before Him to whom we owe
everything—all this (expressed in the language of the
early seventeenth century, at times even with a

certain subtlety characteristic of that age and which we can scarcely now understand)—is clearly revealed in these few pages written simply, spontaneously and just as her pen ran on.

' She had always,' as her first biographer tells us, [4] ' an extraordinary love and hunger for mental prayer, according to the testimony of His Lordship the Bishop of Belley, and as her mind was elevated, her judgement solid and formed by the study of philosophy and wide reading, her heart tender and penetrated with God, she prayed in a strong, sublime and effective manner ; and these dispositions of her soul may be sensibly recognised in the meditations which she left in writing. . . . The great habit she acquired of prayer and retirement was manifested in all her actions by her application to God, which resulted in her always being recollected amidst the diversity and multiplicity of her occupations, by her attention to her vocal prayers, when she remained fixed and motionless before the altar, by her tenderness and love at Holy Communion, after which she was often seen to leave the church with tears in her eyes, and the little handkerchief she made use of was quite saturated with tears ; and finally, by her union and conformity with the Will of God in pains and sickness, when her spirit was ever tranquil and content and during which she never complained, and by the fervour of her spiritual conferences and conversations when she spoke in a moving and effective manner, and as if by outbursts and transports.'

This simple and charming portrait, painted by her first biographer, is certainly that of Saint Vincent's

collaborator during those years of spiritual maturity
to which she had attained, and which were destined
to be so fruitful both for herself and for others.
' Let us live then,' she wrote in one of her meditations, ' as dead in Jesus Christ, and as such let us
make no further resistance to Jesus, act only for
Jesus, have no thoughts save in Jesus, and lastly,
have no life save for Jesus and our neighbour. So
that, in this unitive love, I love all that Jesus loves.'[5]
In another place she writes :[6] ' Oh ! pure Love !
How I love Thee, for Thou art as strong as death !
Separate me from all that is contrary to Thee.' If
she is at home in this lofty spirituality, if she has
mystical flights and lyrical outbursts at the thought
of God and His love, such as all really holy souls
have experienced, yet she always comes back to her
own particular vocation, to the love of Christ in
His poor, in those suffering members who go to make
up His mystical body. That is her way, and she
knew it and was in no danger of mistaking it. ' At
every opportunity of doing good to my neighbour,'
she says, ' I will reflect that for me he has been
substituted in the place of our Lord, by a loving
method known to Himself, which He has taught
my soul to understand and which I cannot express.'

There, in truth, lies the cause, and at the same
time, the nourishment of that devotion and hunger
that need for spending herself for others that
devoured her ; it is always the living Christ whom
she sees in them, and it is He whom she loves in
loving them, and in devoting herself to their service.
Louise de Marillac, moreover, despite the fervour
of her devotion and her ardent piety, never failed to

be the first to give her young community an example
of the sincerest humility and of the most minute
attention to the accomplishment of the least obligations of her state.   Ever the first to be at work, she
would have wished to be treated as the last ; she
reserved to herself, for instance, the task of washing
up the plates and dishes after meals ; she asked
pardon in public from her Daughters for any
failings she might have shown in her dealings with
them ; finally, she made herself responsible for the
faults committed by some of those poor girls, who,
coming from the humblest ranks of society, had not
yet been sufficiently trained.   ' The faults of our
Sisters,' she wrote, ' are only the fruits of the poor
garden of my wretched government.   It is my sins
that have caused them, and it seems to me I deserve
severe punishment for all their failings.'   This profound humility which was perhaps at times a little over-
anxious, and which her spiritual guide always sought
to moderate by re-assuring her and by urging her
not to indulge in too much introspection, nevertheless did not prevent her from ruling her little flock
with combined firmness and good humour.   She
knew how to reprimand strictly on occasion, and at
times, as Saint Vincent remarks, ' mingled a drop
of vinegar with the sweetness of her spirit.'   But
she always remained perfectly simple and natural,[7]
moderating as well as she could, in response to Saint
Vincent's request ' that slight over-seriousness which
was natural to her but which grace had already
mitigated.'   Often enough, indeed, as she once told
her Daughters, she felt, in the midst of those interior
struggles, those battles which every true servant of

God has to wage and of which her director alone held the secret, ' her heart so oppressed that she could scarcely open her mouth. And yet, she added, I try with all my strength to laugh.'[8] Her patience towards the Sisters under her charge was inexhaustible, and it was only at the very last extremity, when it became only too plain that they were unsuited to the work or had no vocation, that she made up her mind to send them away. When any of her companions or Daughters fell ill, she showed them the utmost kindness, care and sympathy, ' remembering that she should be a mother to them and lavishing on them all the attention that was in her power.'

In this light, then, Louise de Marillac is revealed to us at this period in her life, from her letters and those of Saint Vincent, from contemporary documents and from her first biographers. Furthermore, she was more inclined to put herself in the last place, to humble and mortify herself, than were any of her companions (for instance, she wore the old clothes of the community for the sake of example), yet she was quite prepared, whenever the occasion demanded, to use the drops of vinegar, as Saint Vincent remarked, to recall Sisters to their duty, or to make her own reasonable and practical will prevail.

As her inner life was of an elevated order, it eludes, by that very fact, any investigations of it that could be made here ; nevertheless it was perfectly simple. She frequented the Sacraments and practised vocal and mental prayer during those rare moments when she was not engaged in carrying out charitable deeds of every description, in the government of the Sisters (whom she would not allow to be called ' her ' Daughters in her own presence) and in a correspondence that was absolutely essential if the community were to advance in an even and regular manner.   We cannot, however, omit to say something more about the hidden life of Louise de Marillac without incurring the reproach of incompleteness.   She concealed it so well that it can only just be indicated, but it is there we must seek for the solid base on which her works repose, for here, as in human constructions, even if the foundations are hidden from our eyes, they are none the less essential and support the entire building. Before Louise de Marillac became the Sister of Charity whom we know, she had begun by being a true and then a great Christian woman in the widest, fullest and highest sense of the word, and it was only when she had become, without realising it herself, an instrument well tempered by God that she set herself to labour externally for the glory of His name and the welfare of her neighbour.   This is what should never be forgotten when we study the lives of the Saints ; the great works which attract both our eyes and our imaginations only too often lead us to forget that they are first of all Christian men and women, more perfect no doubt than the rest of us, but true Christians before everything else, and that that is the source of their untiring devotedness as well as of their heroic detachment. If the accomplishment of great deeds is granted to them, if true miracles at times are the recompense of their faith, it is always because they are true

Christians, and no one is more astonished, more dismayed even than themselves at the sight of what God has wrought by their means.

That is the common characteristic of all the Saints; it is true that their biographers, perhaps from a secret wish to make them even greater than they are, often conceal this fact beneath the more striking aspects of their lives, but this is sometimes done to the detriment of the faith which would be really and truly strengthened by a remembrance of this truth. For if sanctity is nothing else than the Christian religion practised in perfection, what is Christianity itself except Truth brought down to us from on high by Him who is Truth itself? Now, Louise de Marillac, docile in this to the example and teaching of her guide, S. Vincent de Paul, realised this truth perfectly and bequeathed it as her spirit to her innumerable posterity. Before establishing first one great work, and then several, she was a Christian woman who sought to be nothing else, and if God granted such a surprising fruitfulness to her life, this humbled her first of all. The idea of attributing an iota of the results to herself never even occurred to her. She always remained in her own eyes, as in those of others, the same kind, simple ' Mademoiselle ' who was just attempting to effect some good, even when she could clearly see the ever-increasing success of her charitable enterprises and their marvellous results.

The years we are now considering were, as a matter of fact, very busy: they resemble those harvest-times which poets and painters have commemorated in all countries and ages. In the

K

early months of the year 1641, Louse de Marillac's little band once more changed their place of residence. They returned to Paris and set up their establishment in a small house in the Rue Saint-Laurent, in the Faubourg Saint-Denys, which was quite close to and almost opposite Saint Vincent's priory of Saint-Lazare. The house belonged to him, and at first he let it, and then later, in 1653, sold it to Louise de Marillac and her Daughters. It became the Mother-House of the Sisters, and Louise was scarcely absent from it up to the day of her death. It was here she received the poor refugees who fled to Paris during the wars in Lorraine and also during the civil war of the Fronde, and it was here she definitely organised her institute and watched over its development. The house remained standing until the French Revolution; it was confiscated in 1793 and pulled down, and at the present day, the Boulevard Magenta passes over its site. The lease states that it is ' situated close to and opposite the Church of Saint-Lazare; it consists of three separate groups of buildings side by side, one of which has a courtyard in which there is a stable and a well, and a garden in the rear, the whole being enclosed with walls; in front, there is an open space newly paved and reaching as far as the footpath of the street; it stretches on one side to an open space and a small angular plot of land beside the new Rue Saint-Laurent.'⁹

The whole property was acquired by Louise de Marillac for nine thousand *livres*, the greater part of which sum had been bequeathed by Madame de Goussault. ' It may be said,' as the first biographer of our saint remarks, in his quaint and flowery language,[10] ' that it was here she built a dwelling-house and a sanctuary for charity. Hitherto, she had only afforded it a temporary home liable to change and like unto the tabernacle of Moses which had no stability and was transported from place to place. But in this house she established a fixed and permanent temple for charity, by making it a general place of refuge for all poor persons who were attracted thither from all parts by her reputation, and as it were, a public depôt for most of the alms of Paris which were poured out into the hands of this faithful administrator.'

Once installed in its new home, the ' little Company,' which had hitherto lived in a sort of simple, voluntary association, now became definitely organised as the Society of the Daughters of Charity. It was also at this time that the provisional set of rules drawn up by Louise de Marillac and Vincent de Paul became definitive, almost in the same form and substance as it exists to-day. Here, too, Saint Vincent began to hold those series of conferences which, carefully collected after the meeting was over so as to preserve their original setting, still provide the spiritual food and nourishment of his countless Daughters. Finally, it was in this house that, as we shall presently describe, the first Daughters of Charity just one year later were authorised to pronounce simple vows of poverty, chastity and obedience, to be renewed annually. At a somewhat later period, the little congregation was duly authorised and recognised by the ecclesiastical authorities, and S. Vincent de Paul nominated its first Superior. He was soon replaced by his first companion, Father Portail, whilst Louise de Marillac was appointed Superior-General, taking, at Saint Vincent's suggestion, the title of ' servant of the poor Daughters of Charity, as being more humble and in greater conformity with the office as it actually existed.'

This rapid enumeration suffices to show how these years in the life of Louise de Marillac were fully occupied and what a harvest she reaped. To supply a full and exact account would demand a body of evidence which Louise, faithful in this as in all else to the lesson of Saint Vincent, had less intention than any one to hand on to us. For she had no idea and no intention of establishing a religious order, any more than she had of accomplishing any great work ; she simply wished to do all the good in her power without any sort of display or ostentation whatsoever. That was her sole aim : she was working simply for the glory of God and the welfare of her neighbour without any preconceived plans ; all that followed came ' by way of increase,' as the Scripture says, and what actually did follow was the advent of the Sisters of Charity.

In their fear of setting up anything that might have the semblance of a new religious order, the two founders avoided even the name and outward appearance of nuns. The Sisters were at first ' just good country girls ' who devoted themselves to the service of the poor and sick. The little house in the Rue Saint-Laurent which sheltered those who were undergoing a course of training, became not a novitiate, for that would have conveyed the idea

of a religious congregation, but a ' seminary,' in
which the Sisters of Charity were trained ; their
vocation was tested and they were rendered fit to
carry out their duties efficiently.   The word
' seminary ' was employed and is even employed
at the present day to designate the period of the
Sisters' spiritual formation. As it was essential that
they should have the same form of dress, both as a
defence and a protection, they wore the usual costume of poor peasant girls, a greyish blue robe with
a white collar, and a white kerchief on their head
such as peasant girls then usually wore.   This
kerchief was later on replaced by a white coif or
' cornette ' which is still the head-dress of the Sisters
of Charity.   From the beginning Louise de Marillac
desired to wear the same modest costume as the
other members of her little band, but her perpetual
bad health and the resultant inability to endure
changes of temperature forbade it, and she had to
make use of much warmer clothing in the shape of a
cloak.   Sisters of Charity at the present day wear a
small shawl which is their substitute for Louise de
Marillac's cloak.   Whenever she left home she used
to wear ' gloves and a veil ' as she had been accustomed to do from childhood and as was then customary with persons of the higher classes, but this
was entirely against her own wishes and she only
did so out of obedience and perfect simplicity.[11]
' Her weak health,' says Barbara Bailly, one of the
first Sisters, ' did not allow of her having her head
uncovered, for it made her ill, and so she had to
resume a head-dress.   But she always showed the
greatest desire to dress like the rest, and as her

delicate state of health would not permit it, she regarded herself as being unworthy to be called a Sister of Charity.'

Moreover, it was during this period and in the little house in the Rue Saint-Laurent that Saint Jane Frances de Chantal visited Louise de Marillac and Vincent de Paul. It is a meeting of profound interest in the religious history of that age and one that lends itself to literary or psychological developments, to use the modern phrase, if this were the place to attempt them. 'I had the happiness of seeing Madame de Chantal yesterday,' Louise wrote quite simply to Saint Vincent, 'I do not know what God will do with me who am so unfaithful to him and so full of sins!'[12]

Saint Chantal, who was then seventy years old, died shortly afterwards; she had come to Paris to pay a last visit to her daughters there. Before returning home, she had gone to see in the little house in the Faubourg Saint-Denys a work which was just beginning and which in a manner realised the primitive idea of her own institute, and to give, as it were, her blessing to it. For, in the mysterious designs of Providence, the original intention of the Daughters of the Visitation had been to visit the sick outside the boundaries of their own convent and to nurse them either in their own homes or in hospitals, as well as to practise the spiritual and corporal works of mercy. Thus, what had been Saint Chantal's primary intention and what she had to abandon, was destined to be effected by the Daughters of Charity of Louise de Marillac, though they had never meant to do so, and were driven, so to say, by the force of circumstances. In this way they had merited, as Saint Vincent once remarked to them in a conference, ' the crown which God had destined for the Daughters of Saint Mary,' and the future was to show that he had judged rightly.[13] But if this were to be so, it was essential that the work should be so well organised as to be able to exist by itself, independently of its founders. Louise de Marillac, notwithstanding her humility which always inclined her to think that she was unworthy of founding anything whatever, on account of her manifold sins, was compelled to recognise this fact. She fell in with Saint Vincent's ideas, and he began to draw up a uniform set of regulations, not to say a regular rule, for all the different houses of the Sisters. Moreover, with that end in view, he commenced, as we have said, to deliver the admirable series of conferences into which he threw his whole soul and his love of God and his neighbour. ' Up to this,' he says at the beginning of the second conference,[14] ' my engagements prevented me from helping you : I often have attacks of remorse of conscience and they have made me resolve to speak to you henceforward every fortnight. We must look over your order of day and arrange that wherever you may be, you shall all carry out your religious exercises, your prayers, vocal and mental, your examinations of conscience and your meals at the same time. . . . Humble yourselves greatly, my dear Sisters, and strive to render yourselves perfect and to become saints. For it is not to be hoped that those who will come after you and who will model themselves on your example, will be better than you : as a rule, everything produces its like. So take care then not to debase your state, or rather, to allow it to be dishonoured, by leaving behind you, and on account of your example, Sisters who are not worthy of such a high office.'

Faithful to his programme, Vincent de Paul developed in a series of conferences, which have remained the greatest treasure of the Daughters of Charity, the spirit and the rules of 'the little Company' as they were to be observed in all places, and in accordance with the special works to be carried on by the different communities.

There can be no question of giving a detailed analysis of these conferences which are replete with the spirit that animated the saint who delivered them ; it suffices to say that it is in accordance with their teaching that the true Sister of Charity such as we see her at the present day is formed. She avoids in particular, as ' her dear Father ' urged her, and as ' Mademoiselle ' gave her the example, ' all over-tenderness of body and mind in her own regard,' and she seeks to practise in reality ' contempt for the spirit of the world.' Speaking of this subject on one occasion, Saint Vincent said :[15] ' Oh ! yes, there are some Sisters amongst you who afford me great consolation in this respect. And when, for instance, I meet them in the streets carrying a basket on their backs, I cannot express the joy it gives me. Oh ! blessed be God for it.' It was Louise who, at the request of her spiritual father, selected the subject of the conference and it was also she who carefully noted down its chief points.

' I trust, sir,' she says in one of her letters,[16]

' that our Sisters will make good use of the instruction which your Charity has given us to-day. Their hearts are filled with a desire to do so, and they would clearly wish to remember it always ; this leads me to request you very humbly to send us the little memorandum of the points in your possession. It seems to me that it will help me to remember a good part of what our good God has told us, speaking through your mouth. Shall I never, before I die, be in the state which God, in His love, demands of me ? Do me the charity of thinking over this a little, and pray consider what are my failings so that I may not at the hour of death suffer the confusion I deserve for all my unfaithfulness to the designs of God, especially when He will demand of me an account of all that has happened since His goodness gave me the grace of being, Most Honoured Father, your humblest and most obliged servant,

LOUISE DE MARILLAC.'

These conferences which are so simple, so vivid, so filled with the love of God that replenished the heart of Saint Vincent, exercised a profound influence on the formation of the first Sisters of Charity and were of the utmost importance for the establishment of the institute. Hence, it was Vincent de Paul himself who one day suggested the idea that the Sisters should take vows. ' A few days ago,' he remarked in 1639, during one of the first conferences,[17] ' I had the unspeakable consolation of hearing the vows of the Hospitallers read out ; I must let you hear them too. Here are the terms of their vows : " I, brother so and so, vow and promise to God to observe all my life, poverty, chastity, obedience, and *to serve our lords*, the poor." You see, my dear Sisters, how pleasing it is to God to serve His beloved members in this way.' Saint Vincent spoke with so much fervour that, as the account of the conference goes on to say, ' some of our Sisters, being deeply moved, asked if they might not make a similar act in the Company. His Charity made the following reply : " Yes, certainly, my Daughters, with this difference, that as the vows of these religious are solemn, they can only be dispensed from them by the Pope, whereas we can be dispensed by the bishop from the vows which we make." ' He added that it would be much better for them not to make vows at all than to make them with the intention of obtaining a dispensation from them subsequently. The question was asked whether the Sisters might not make these vows individually, and as their devotion suggested. ' His charity said that it was most essential to guard against this, but that those who felt such a desire should tell the superior, and then rest content, whether permission was granted to make vows, or whether it was refused.' . . . ' After which, M. Vincent, raising his eyes to Heaven, pronounced the following prayer : " O my God ! let us give ourselves entirely to Thee, grant us the grace to live and die in the perfect practice of holy poverty ; I implore this grace for all our Sisters, absent and present. Do you not desire this, my Daughters ? Grant us moreover the grace to live chastely and to obey perfectly. I implore Thy mercy for all the Sisters of Charity and for myself. We also offer ourselves to Thee, O my

God, during the whole course of our lives, for our lords the poor. We implore this grace from Thee by Thy holy love. Do you not also desire that, my dear daughters " ' ? All the Sisters manifested their desire with great devotion, and all knelt down. Saint Vincent gave them his blessing as usual, asking God to grant them the grace to accomplish His designs in their regard. He then explained to them that they must not aspire to ' the name of religious,' in the sense given to the word at that time, ' because religious implies a cloister, the grille and the office in common, all of which are incompatible with their vocation.' S. Vincent de Paul, far from being in any hurry, and in accordance with his usual custom, allowed some time to pass before he gave permission to his Daughters to carry out their good resolutions. No doubt he wished to try them, and to see, as we should say to-day, how matters exactly stood.

It was only two years later that Louise de Marillac was authorised by him, as we have seen, to allow four of her Daughters to carry out their desires, and to bind themselves for one year to observe the three vows of poverty, chastity, and obedience. The engagement was taken for one year only, and was renewable annually.

On March 25, 1642, the anniversary of the day on which Louise de Marillac eight years previously had given herself to God and consecrated herself to works of charity, four of her Daughters took the temporary vows of which we have spoken. Louise wished to unite herself with them, and to renew her own engagements whilst they were making theirs.

Everything passed off without any ceremony or display, as the first life of Mademoiselle Le Gras informs us when it refers to the four Sisters who were permitted to pronounce annual promises, that is, simple vows. 'Having disposed themselves by Holy Communion, and having heard Mass with that intention, immediately after the elevation of the Sacred Host, the four Sisters pronounced in the silence of their consciences the formula of engagement which has since been preserved in this Company.' The last lines of this formula were, it is said, written out in Louise de Marillac's own hand on the original copy which still exists. 'I, the undersigned, in the presence of God, renew my baptismal vows and I make vows of poverty, chastity and obedience to the Venerable General of the Priests of the Mission, in the Company of the Daughters of Charity, with the intention of devoting myself for a year to the corporal and spiritual service of the sick poor our true masters ; and this I do, relying on the assistance of God, which I ask from Him through Jesus crucified, and by the intercession of the Blessed Virgin.' The whole ceremony took place in silence and recollection, and nothing seemed changed as far as externals went.

Nevertheless, this date, March 25, 1642, marked the definite establishment of the Company of the Sisters of Charity, and Louise de Marillac's work was now founded. Henceforward Sisters began to join the Company as they would have entered any other congregation, and the numbers kept on increasing. The annual vows (which seemed at first to be just a precaution and an evidence of good will, from the fact that they were renewed only every year) formed the little Company into a living compact society, which, though it always avoided and refused to accept the name of an 'order' or 'a religion,' to employ the word then in use, was none the less a united and firmly established whole. What was said of another celebrated Order which also did not make perpetual vows is applicable to the Sisters of Charity: 'As God has so willed it, it does not proceed from us so much as it does from others.'

So each member of the 'little Company,' mother and Daughters, worked together with greater zeal than ever, visiting the sick, nursing them in their own homes, notwithstanding the fear of contagion and at the risk of their lives, with an ardour and a charity that nothing could weary. Vincent de Paul, like many another, was deeply moved at the sight and saw in it a mark of divine protection. The providential usefulness of the new Congregation was henceforth well established in his mind, and an event occurred, in 1644, that served to convince him even more fully.

On the eve of Pentecost, during one of those retreats which Louise de Marillac made regularly from Ascension Thursday to Whit-Sunday, she was very nearly killed together with several of her Daughters. 'Mademoiselle,' wrote Saint Vincent, 'was in the common room when the main beam broke. A Sister who had heard it cracking went to tell her that the room was not safe. She paid no heed to it. Nevertheless, an older Sister having come to tell her the same thing she deferred to her age and withdrew. She was scarcely three paces away, at the next door, when the beam broke and the ceiling fell. Do you not believe that that did not happen without a special intervention of God?' Vincent de Paul himself was to have held a meeting of the Ladies of Charity on that very day in the same room. ' But God,' he adds in the letter from which we have quoted, ' brought about a certain business which interfered with this arrangement and which prevented all the Ladies from meeting there. And if this had not happened, we should all have been crushed beneath the weight of the ceiling, for the cracking of the beam would not have been heard amidst all the noise of the assembly, nor could the Sister have warned us, because she would not have ventured to enter the room as we should have been there.' Saint Vincent, who knew Mademoiselle Le Gras too well not to fear lest she might be tempted to attribute the cause of this accident to her own sins, hastened to write and tell her to be on her guard against such an idea. ' You have,' he wrote, ' a new motive for loving God more than ever on account of what has happened, seeing that He has preserved you as the apple of His eye from an accident in which you might have been crushed under the ruins. I have told the members of our Company and we have all returned thanks to God for having, in His amiable providence, averted such a disaster. With God's help, I hope to have the happiness of seeing you here soon, if you come to Vespers, or in your own house, to pay my respects and to bid you good-day.' Louise de Marillac, on her side, wrote in her note-book the following touching lines on her providential escape. We cannot refrain from quoting them here, as her whole soul is revealed in them. ' The day and the hour in which our good God has permitted us to recognise his Divine Providence, by the very remarkable event of the collapse of our ceiling, has once more brought before my eyes the interior change I experienced when His goodness granted me light and guidance on the great difficulties and anxieties of mind which I then experienced. I thought that our whole family should have a special devotion to the feast of Pentecost and a total dependence on Divine Providence, and that in a most particular and special manner. It then seemed to me that something great was being effected for the establishment of this little family. I understood that this accident, which should rather be called a grace, should be an intimation to our most honoured Father that a close union is essential between His Institute and our Community, according to God's will, as they have interests in common.

' And although, wretched as I am, I should have recognised that all this had happened on account of my sins, such an idea never even occurred to me either at the time or afterwards ; but I have always said, and still more believed in my heart, that it was a grace from God, wrought for an end we know not, and that God had in this way asked something both from them and from us, and I trust His goodness will make this known to our most honoured Father.'

Hence she desired, in the ardour of her faith and gratitude, that in future and for ever the anniversary of this day on which God had so clearly shown herself and her Daughters such visible protection, should be celebrated annually. With that in view, she asked permission for them and for herself to go to Holy Communion every month on that date, and also to make a spiritual retreat from Ascension Thursday to Pentecost. ' I should like with all my heart to give, and to have given, to God much glory so as to correspond with the design He has had in permitting what has happened to us ; and on that account, I shall try to remember it all my life, and to thank God for the interior thoughts and feelings He then communicated to me.'[18]

On another occasion, a Sister attached to the ' Charity ' in the parish of Saint-Sulpice, was visiting a sick man in the Faubourg Saint-Germain, when she too escaped by God's special protection from an accident that threatened her life. Carrying her pot of soup, she was going upstairs to bring the patient his dinner, when, on reaching the landing between the first and second story of the house, she heard a water-carrier who was in front of her, crying out in terror : ' We are lost,' whilst at the same moment the building began to sway. The terrified Sister had just time to squeeze herself into an angle of the staircase before the whole building collapsed, crushing and burying from thirty-five to forty people in the ruins. The poor Sister, thus left suspended, as it were, between heaven and earth, was observed by the crowd who had arrived attracted by the noise. Some stretched out a pole to her, whilst others, taking off their cloaks spread them beneath her. Relying on God's goodness, and only after she had carefully fastened her soup-pot to the pole, she threw herself down on the cloths stretched beneath her and rose up without having suffered any injury. She at once picked up her soup-pot and notwithstanding her emotion, proceeded on her round of charitable visits. 'We should believe,' said Saint Vincent to his Daughters, ' that it was Angels who preserved her. Oh ! what a protection ! Do you think it was just by chance that she escaped without injury ? Oh ! no, no, no. The whole thing is miraculous : God ordained all that to let your Company know what care He is taking of you. . . . Oh ! my Daughters, what reason have you not for trusting yourselves to God ! We read in history that a man was killed in the open country by a tortoise that an eagle let fall on his head, and we see to-day Daughters of Charity coming without a scratch from beneath the ruins of a house that had collapsed to its very foundations. Is not that a sensible proof by which God lets you all know that you are as dear to Him as the apple of His eye ? Oh ! my Daughters ! Rest assured that, provided you preserve a holy confidence in your hearts, God will always preserve you no matter where you may be.'

Saint Vincent, then, more and more convinced that the work on which Louise de Marillac was engaged had been willed by God, finally allowed himself to be persuaded by his prudent fellow-worker that the time had now come for him to procure for it ' that more solid establishment ' which she had so long and so silently hoped and prayed for.

L

NOTES ON CHAPTER V

[1] Baunard, *op. cit.*, 62 *et alias*.
[2] *Letters of S. Vincent de Paul*, p. 130.
[3] *Op. cit.*, p. 209.
[4] *Vie de Louise de Marillac*, par Gobillon, p. 69.
[5] Louise de Marillac, *Écrits et Pensées*, p. 52.
[6] *Op. cit.*, p. 67.
[7] *Vie de Mademoiselle Le Gras*, par la Comtesse de Richemont, p. 196.
[8] Baunard, *op. cit.*, p. 478.
[9] Baunard, *op. cit.*, p. 266.
[10] Gobillon, *op. cit.*, p. 85.
[11] Baunard, *op. cit.*, p. 298.
[12] *Lettres de Louise de Marillac à M. Vincent*, p. 75.
[13] *Conférences de Saint Vincent de Paul*, Conf. LXI, p. 331.
[14] *Op. cit.*, Conf. II, p. 7.
[15] *Op. cit.*, Conf. XV, p. 63.
[16] *Lettres de Louise de Marillac à Saint Vincent de Paul*, Letter LXXIX, p. 119.
[17] *Conférences de Saint Vincent de Paul*, Conf. III, p. 112.
[18] Louise de Marillac, *Écrits*, p. 184, No. 93.

CHAPTER VI

THE DEFINITIVE ESTABLISHMENT OF 'THE LITTLE
COMPANY' — 'MADEMOISELLE' AND HER
DAUGHTERS—THE HOSPITAL OF THE HOLY NAME
OF JESUS—THE GENERAL HOSPITAL—THE MENTAL
HOSPITAL CALLED 'THE LITTLE HOUSES'
1644-1655

THE 'Little Company' which had grown up
so quietly and had now begun to branch out
on all sides, had not yet received any official approbation or recognition. If it were to prove lasting
and capable of resisting trials and changes, it was
essential that it should be recognised and approved
both by the King, the Archbishop of Paris, and
lastly, by the Pope. Otherwise it would have run
the risk of wearing away, so to speak, as the years
went by, owing to the weakness of some and the
ill-will of others, for these are never wanting in
human affairs however good or useful they may be.
S. Vincent de Paul, with that practical good sense
which is the most outstanding feature of his character, fully realised this. Hence, urged by Louise de
Marillac who was increasingly insistent, he thought
the time had at length come to have the Society, as
it was then constituted, approved first by ecclesiastical, and then by royal authority. But here again

he showed no haste, no over-eagerness, nothing human, as he would have said, in the execution of this design, essential though it was if the work they had begun were to continue. Mademoiselle Le Gras, who understood him so well, did not, as a matter of fact, urge him unduly : she followed his instructions with docility. Nevertheless, she had her own ideas both as to the form the new Institute should take, and especially as to the authority it should be subject to. She put them before her spiritual guide with the utmost freedom, and with the help of Providence, succeeded in having her own way. The independence of spirit combined with the most complete deference on the one side, and on the other the free admission, as the most natural thing in the world, of a different standpoint from her whom Saint Vincent regarded as, and who actually was, his collaborator, is much too honourable to both Vincent de Paul and Louise de Marillac for us not to refer to the matter. This state of affairs arose in connection with the approbation of the new Congregation.

In 1645, S. Vincent de Paul, in his desire to give his Daughters ' a more solid foundation,' drew up a memoir addressed to John Francis de Gondi, Archbishop of Paris, in which he asks for the approbation of the Company so that its perpetuity may be secured. ' For,' said he, ' works concerned with God's service come to an end, as a rule, with those who have begun them, if there be no spiritual bond uniting those persons who have devoted themselves to the work.'

The Sisters' rule of life was added to this memorandum. He therefore requested the Archbishop to give this approbation to the rules which were forwarded with the petition, and in accordance with which 'the Sisters have lived up to the present and propose so to live for the future,' and also to establish them as a society under the name of Daughters and Widows of Charity, Servants of the Poor. Saint Vincent submitted the documents to Mademoiselle Le Gras and asked for her opinion. 'Mademoiselle,' he wrote,[1] 'enclosed is the memoir for the establishment of the Daughters. It contains three points : 1. The manner in which Providence has brought them into existence ; 2. Their mode of life up to the present ; 3. The rules of their confraternity or association. . . . You will, however, read and comment on the said document. I have omitted a number of things I might have said about yourself. Let us leave it to our Lord to say it to the whole world some day, and let us hide ourselves in the meantime.' Louise de Marillac obeyed ; she read the petition carefully and made some comments, especially on the omission of the title 'Daughters of Charity' on which she insisted, and which afterwards prevailed. But as her opinion had been asked for, despite her wonted modesty, she was not afraid to give the freest expression to her views on a more important point.

In the petition and memorandum drawn up by Saint Vincent he stated that the Archbishop of Paris should nominate an ecclesiastical superior for the Company, who should depend entirely on 'the Ordinary,' to employ the technical term. Now, the new Company had hitherto been under the direction

of the ' Priests of the Mission ' which Saint Vincent
had recently founded, and it had found in them a
support and assistance which had proved to be of
the utmost value.   Louise de Marillac knew this
better than anyone else, and she saw with her usual
clearsightedness the necessity of this relationship for
the future and for the development of the Sisters of
Charity.   She therefore felt that she was quite at
liberty to put her ideas before Saint Vincent de Paul
on the subject, and to endeavour to bring him round
to her own way of thinking.

' Sir,' she wrote to him,[2] ' may not the expression
of such absolute dependence on his Grace be a
source of injury to us in the future, since it allows
us to be withdrawn from the direction of the
Superior-General of the Mission ? Is it not essential,
Sir, that your Charity should be appointed perpetual director by this document, and as for the
rules that are to be laid down for us, is it His Grace's
intention that they should be those set out subsequently in the petition ? In the name of God,
Sir, do not allow anything to be done which might
even in the slightest degree remove the Company
from the government which God has given it ; for
you know quite well that at once it would cease to
be what it has been so far. And the sick poor would
be no longer nursed, and I really do believe that the
Will of God would no longer be observed amongst
us.' S. Vincent de Paul, with his usual humility,
did not think he was bound to take account of these
suggestions which might possibly have seemed to
be to the advantage of his own Congregation.
He did not alter the petition.

The Archbishop's approbation, though assured in advance, was not given for a considerable period, and it was only a year subsequently, on November 20, 1646, that it was granted. This approbation was immediately sanctioned by Royal Letters-Patent, and nothing more remained to be done before its promulgation than what seemed to be the observance of a mere formality, its registration by the Parliament. So, without waiting for the observance of the formality, S. Vincent de Paul thought he should announce the good news to his Daughters at a conference in which he read the rules and statutes of their Institute.[3] When he had read out the article in which it was laid down that the Superioress should be elected for three years, and was eligible for re-election for a further period of three years 'but no longer,' he went on to add : ' But this of course shall not be in force until after the death of Mademoiselle.' At these words, Louise de Marillac knelt down and besought Saint Vincent to put the rule in force immediately. ' Your Sisters and I,' he replied, ' should pray to God to preserve your life for many long years, as He ordinarily preserves by extraordinary means, those who are necessary for the accomplishing of His works. Furthermore, Mademoiselle, if you will only consider the matter carefully, you will see that for the last ten years you have not been kept alive by any ordinary means.'

Everything therefore seemed to have been definitely settled, and Mademoiselle Le Gras no doubt had resigned herself to the abandonment of her own ideas. As, however, the royal approbation and the registration by the Parliament of the Archbishop's Letters-Patent were still delayed, Louise wrote to Saint Vincent of the efforts she was making to have the matter terminated by means of the new Procurator-General, Nicholas Fouquet. In 1650, the latter succeeded Mesliand in that office, and all the documents in the case were submitted to him with a view to registration.[4]   In 1650, she wrote to Saint Vincent, ' Yesterday I went by chance to see the Procurator-General who did me the honour of receiving me in the most courteous fashion.   He said to me at once that I had doubtless come about a matter which he had in hand.   I told him I had come to refresh his memory on the subject. He asked me if we meant to be regulars or seculars. I informed him that we intended to be only seculars. He said to me " that would be unexampled."   I referred him to the Daughters of Madame de Villeneuve, and proved to him that they went about everywhere.   He declared that he did not disapprove of our design, and said many kind things about the Company, adding that a matter of such importance certainly deserved careful thought and reflection. I let him see how pleased I was by his attitude and begged him *if the whole affair did not deserve to, or should not, be continued, that he should destroy it com- pletely, but that if it were good, we begged him to establish it solidly,* and I said that it was this idea which had led us to make our attempt for at least the past twelve or fifteen years, during which, by God's grace, *nothing inconvenient had occurred.*   He said to me : " Let me think over it, not for months, but for a few weeks."   He was kind enough to accompany

us to the carriage which was waiting in the courtyard. But he manifested the greatest good-will in
our regard and begged us to present you with his most
humble salutations, saying that he would be a usurer
if he accepted the most humble thanks we paid him
for the honour he had done all our Sisters whenever
they had ventured to approach him in their needs,
both for the poor convicts and for little children.'

But when the Procurator-General was prepared
to carry out his promise and enquire into the matter
more closely, a strange and unexpected incident
occurred which once more opened up the whole
question. The Royal Letters-Patent, which contained the ecclesiastical approbation of the Company
and which should have been registered by the Parliament, had gone astray and could not be found.
' The said approbation,'[5] it is stated later, at the head
of the new Letters that were granted, ' which was
attached to the Letters-Patent it pleased His Majesty
to grant, and which was also attached to those
addressed to the Parliament for registration, has
unfortunately been mislaid by the secretary of
Procurator Mesliand. The secretary subsequently
died without the said approbation to the said
Letters-Patent having been discovered, notwithstanding all possible diligent search of the person
now setting forth the matter, either amongst the
papers of the said Procurator Mesliand or those of
his secretary or at the residence of the present
Procurator-General and his substitutes.' The whole
affair had to be begun all over again, for despite all
the searching for the lost documents, they were
never discovered.

There could no longer be any question of a mere formality and the business was bound to drag on for a considerable period, for Government offices were then very slow to act, even if a trifle more expeditious than those of our own day. Moreover, the times were very disturbed : Louis XIII died, the civil war of the Fronde broke out, so that the whole matter remained in suspense for a long time. Mademoiselle Le Gras, who had thought it her duty to abandon her own ideas when faced with an accomplished fact, now considered she was at liberty to resume them when she saw an opportunity arising in this unsuspected fashion, for her to bring them forward again. Furthermore, the manner in which things were going had already begun to show that she was right. With a perfect liberty and candour which do as much honour to herself as to S. Vincent de Paul to whom she wrote, she set to work to bring him round to her own ideas on the constitution of the ' little Company.' On November 20, 1647, she wrote :[6] ' It seems to me, Sir, that God bestowed a great peace and tranquillity on my soul whilst I was at prayer, imperfect as it was on my part. The subject of my prayers was the necessity of the Company of the Daughters of Charity being under the permanent government which Divine Providence has already given them both in spiritual and temporal matters. During my prayer, it seems to me I heard that it would prove to be more advantageous to God's glory if the Company perished entirely than if it were under any other direction, for it seems that such a state of affairs would be contrary to the Will of God. And the proofs of this are, that there is reason to think that God inspires and makes known His will for the perfection of those works which His goodness desires to accomplish, and it is in the beginning that He makes known His designs. And you know, Sir, that in the beginning of this Company, it was proposed that its temporal possessions, in case it failed through maladministration, should revert to the Mission, and be employed for the instruction of countryfolk. . . . I trust, therefore, that if your Charity has heard our Lord say what it seems to me He said to you, something like what He said to Saint Peter, namely, that it was upon you He wished to build the Company, then you will continue the service He asks of you, namely, the teaching of little ones and the comforting of the sick.'

Over and over again, during the following years whilst things were at a standstill, she returned to the charge : she did so with an insistence very unlike her usual conduct but which certainly proceeded from the depth and sincerity of her conviction. On July 5, 1651, she wrote to Saint Vincent ,[7]

' MY MOST HONOURED FATHER,

The manner in which Divine Providence has decreed that I should address you on all occasions has had this result, namely, that when it is a question of carrying out God's holy Will, I should speak to you very simply on certain necessary things, which we have learned by experience might interfere with the building up of the Company of the Daughters of Charity ; if indeed God has not made known that He wishes it to be entirely destroyed on account of the general and particular faults that have been clearly observable in it for some years, of which I believe, in truth and before God, I am the chief cause, wretched as I am, on account of the bad example I have given, my negligence, and the little zeal I have shown in performing my duty ; and that is one of the greatest necessities to be provided for as regards the future, I mean the appointment, from the present moment, of someone who will give better example.

' A second necessity is that the mode of life should be set down in writing, distributed in those places where there are Sisters capable of reading it, that it should be reverently preserved, and that copies of these rules should neither be shown or given to outsiders. And that each Sister in the Company may know the Rule, it could be read, as far as Paris is concerned, every month by the Sister Servant (Louise de Marillac is here referring to herself) to the Sisters of the parishes who could meet here for that purpose, one half every fortnight and the other half a fortnight later. And as for Sisters in the country, in places where it may not be deemed advisable to give it to them, either because they do not know how to read sufficiently well, or because one cannot fully rely on their discretion, the Rule might be read during the visitation, and when they come here.

' And as there may always be some uncultured minds in the Company, and as knowledge leads to action, it will be necessary that on each point of the rule an explanation should be given of the intention with which it should be carried out.'

' It may be supposed that the mind's natural weakness and fickleness needs to be supported by the sight of some solid establishment, if it is to be helped to surmount the temptations which arise against one's vocation. And the foundation of this establishment without such support would seem to be impossible, nor could the said Company subsist, or God be glorified by it as he apparently desires, for it is absolutely essential that the said Company be erected under the title of Company or Confraternity, entirely submitted to and dependent on the venerable guidance of the most honoured General of the venerable Priests of the Mission, with the consent of their Company, so that, being thus associated with it, the Company (of the Daughters of Charity) may share in the good it is doing, and in order that the Divine goodness through the merits of Jesus Christ and the prayers of the Blessed Virgin may grant it the grace to live in the spirit in which God in His goodness animates the said honourable Congregation.'

' These, my most honoured Father, are my ideas which I have not ventured to conceal from you, submitting them entirely to the judgement which God may desire your charity to form on them, as His goodness has given me the grace so to do for the last twenty-six years, ever since His mercy placed me under your holy guidance to accomplish his most holy Will, for He placed me, my most honoured Father, in a state in which He knows I should remain for the whole course of my life, etc.'

Saint Vincent who, as we have seen, had at first turned a deaf ear to Louise de Marillac, allowed

himself in the end to be shaken and then convinced
by the motives which his humble protagonist did
not fear to put before him with the utmost freedom,
on the necessity of arriving at a definitive establishment and one that by its very constitution should
remove it from the dangers of change and variation.
On November 25, 1651, Mademoiselle Le Gras
even sent Saint Vincent a sort of reasoned statement
in which the motives 'for' and 'against' the
definitive establishment of the 'Little Company'
are set out.[8] ' My own wretchedness and knowledge
of the opposition I offer to the diffusion of God's
grace on the Company,' she says in the beginning,
' have often led me to think that, for the perfection
of its existence, it would be desirable that somebody
else should take my place, who by the example of
her virtues and fidelity in the observance of the rules
might train all the Daughters of Charity in the formation of good habits, and through want of such a
person, it has often occurred to me that Providence
has deferred its definite establishment.

' In the first place, the reasons which have
frequently led me to doubt whether God really
wishes its establishment are : first, the premature
deaths of many good subjects who might have done
much to sustain it ; second, that if the Daughters
saw themselves definitely established, they might
not raise themselves to a holier state than that in
which they now are, and might not carry out their
duties properly ; a third and a fourth reason is the
experience we have had of three or four Sisters who
left the Company with the intention of getting
married, and who consequently suggested the same

idea to others. Now, such ideas border closely on impurity which is a crime that would utterly ruin the Company if it were to exist in it, for the Company should be established with the design of honouring our Lord and the Blessed Virgin who are purity itself. A final reason is to be found in some special failings of our Sisters, such as their slight progress in perfection, especially in the mortification of the senses and the passions.

'On the other hand, what might lead one to think that God does will its establishment, is the excellence of the work in itself, and the blessings His mercy has bestowed on it up to the present; secondly, the action of Divine Providence in guiding and forming it in all its parts; thirdly the liberty its superiors enjoy of removing subjects who might injure it; and also the liberty each individual enjoys of departing. . . . And the strongest motive for believing in the necessity of definitely establishing the Company is that if it were not done now by the person whom God has made use of to bring it into existence, it is not to be expected that his successors would ever venture to do so. I beseech the goodness of God to continue His light and guidance on His work, to root out all that might hinder its progress, and to make His will clear on this matter to those who may wish to be associated with it. I have written at too great length, and very humbly ask pardon for having done so.'

Some difficulties arose about this time in a few of the provincial 'charities' as to what exactly were their proper functions, and this fact supported Louise de Marillac's contentions. They helped to bring Saint Vincent round to her views, and he fell in with her wishes so that in the new petition he asked that the Company of the Daughters of Charity should always depend on the Superior of the Priests of the Mission. So Mademoiselle Le Gras had her way, thanks to the strange and one might say providential disappearance of the first documents relating to the authorisation of her congregation.

But this was the period of the civil war of the Fronde, and the business, of necessity, dragged on slowly, so that it was only in 1655 that Cardinal de Retz, who had succeeded his uncle as Archbishop of Paris, sent from Rome, where he had gone to attend a Conclave, the new letters of authorisation. They were dated January 18, 1655, and addressed to ' our dear and well-beloved Vincent de Paul.' The letters were exactly the same as the earlier ones that had gone astray save for that one point on which Louise de Marillac had set her heart, for they state expressly, after relating the loss of the first documents, that ' this is why the said petitioner has been obliged to have recourse to us, that we may be pleased to approve, for the future, the said Company, and to bestow power on his successors in the office of General to guide the said confraternity under our authority and jurisdiction and that of our successors the Archbishops of Paris, as it is a work for the glory of God and the great solace and comfort of our neighbour. . . . For these motives, and desiring to favour such a good work, and considering that the best means for uniting together and perpetuating the said Daughters and widows, in some form of society or confraternity distinct from that of the said

Ladies of Charity, we have therefore erected and do erect afresh by these presents, the said Daughters in our diocese into a confraternity or special society, under the title of *Servants of the Poor of Charity*, on condition that it shall be and shall remain in perpetuity under our authority and dependent on our successors the Archbishops of Paris. And as God has blessed the efforts made by our aforesaid dear and well-beloved Vincent de Paul for the success of this pious design, *we hereby confer on him and entrust him with the government of the said society and confraternity for the course of his life ; and after him on his successors in the office of Superior-General of the Congregation of the Mission.*'

In this way, the business was at last concluded, and the constitution of the Company of the ' Sisters of Charity ' definitively established under the guidance of the Priests of the Mission, as Louise de Marillac, who may now be rightly called their foundress and mother, had so ardently desired. Henceforward, the work was established and well established, armed to resist the assaults of time and those trials which will never be wanting to all really good works such as are worthy of being offered as a sacrifice to Him who sacrificed Himself for us. If we have considered it our duty to relate in greater detail than such a brief biography might have seemed to warrant, this whole story of the constitution of the Order on which Vincent de Paul and Louise de Marillac were divided, it is because we believed that this episode serves to reveal each of them more clearly. We see Saint Vincent de Paul listening, without any preconceived ideas or personal bias, to

M

her views, and at first showing himself unwilling to adopt them; then, when he had been fully convinced, freely accepting them, while Louise de Marillac on the other hand, without for a moment forgetting that she is addressing her Superior, sets out her own ideas with a frankness and freedom untroubled by any vanity or infatuation, prepared to sacrifice them to obedience, but persevering quite simply in her attempt to have them accepted, in as far as obedience permitted and even obliged her so to act. Both saints have no other aim, object, or desire than the glory of God and the welfare of the poor. It is one of those noble Christian conflicts between two great souls, which supply us with one of the grandest spectacles that poor human nature can present and which console us for those it usually affords even when there is question of persons who are, or think themselves, great.

There is just one other feature which serves to complete the true portrait of Louise de Marillac and which shows her to us as she actually was at this period of her life, and it is this, that far from allowing herself to be absorbed by her preoccupations with the definitive establishment of her work during the years in which we have just now seen her labouring so consistently to effect it, she was, on the contrary, more active and harder at work than during any other period of her whole life. Despite her ever-failing health, which frequently compelled her to cease working for some time, she still devoted herself to her charitable toil, to the care of the sick, to the supervision of works already founded or to the preparations for new ones, to the training of new arrivals amongst the Sisters, with an ever-renewed ardour and perseverance; she combined with her love for the poor and for little ones a devotion that was at once tender and strong, broad, kindly and gracious, yet of an unshakable firmness. In this she imitated the characteristic piety of her master, S. Vincent de Paul, and through him, of S. Francis de Sales, 'the blessed Bishop of Geneva' as he was then called, and her Daughters, in their turn, have inherited this type of devotion from her. To our great regret we have not sufficient space at our disposal to follow her closely during those years which saw the definitive formation of her Company, and we can only just mention, in passing, some of the works with which they were filled.

In 1646, after an attempt to establish the Sisters in the hospital at Mans had fallen through, Mademoiselle Le Gras set out with some Sisters for Nantes, where, on the contrary, they proved a wonderful success in the beginning, and did not at first 'encounter any thorns,' as she wrote to Saint Vincent. Later on, the Sisters had to endure trials and tribulations of all sorts, and were submitted to a number of annoying experiences from which their Mother suffered at a distance even more than if she had been actually on the spot. Then the establishment of the Foundling Hospital in the Castle of Bicêtre entailed more hard work and anxiety. This new form of charity, established many years previously, had rapidly developed; but despite subsidies from Louise XIII and Anne of Austria, the expenses were very heavy, and the undertaking was just barely able to struggle along. In 1647, the

Ladies of Charity who were specially concerned with the work, obtained the Castle of Bicêtre from the Queen for the use of the Foundlings, as the house they had hitherto occupied had by this become much too small. Louise de Marillac viewed this change with anxiety for it necessitated heavy expenditure, and on account of its distance from Paris and the bad state of the roads, proved most fatiguing for the Sisters.

Her anxiety was only too well founded; the resources at her disposal, never very abundant, were constantly diminishing, and the expenses, on the other hand, kept on mounting day by day. ' Experience has shown us,' she remarked in a letter,[9] ' that it was not without cause I feared the house at Bicêtre, and the Ladies of Charity are asking our Sisters to accomplish impossibilities. They have selected for their quarters, tiny rooms, in which the air will be foul, and have left the large rooms empty; but our poor Sisters have not dared to say a word.' And in another letter she says :[10] ' I am very much afraid we shall have to abandon the service of those poor little children. The Will of God be done!' But Louise de Marillac was not a woman who could easily be discouraged, and like her spiritual guide, she well knew how to go on day by day, hoping for everything from God's Providence. They had recourse to the Queen, to the Chancellor, Séguier, to the Procurator-General, and then, during the Fronde, some of the children were brought back to Paris. By means of hard work, economy and privations, the work was successfully carried on during those troubled years.

But towards the end of 1649, things were going so badly that even Mademoiselle Le Gras herself had been forced to think that the enterprise would have to be utterly abandoned. In her distress, she begged Saint Vincent to present a petition to the first President of the Parliament 'to have her relieved of the duty of receiving the Foundlings, and to entrust it to whomsoever he may think fit. . . .' 'I am beginning to think,' she said at the end of her letter, 'that this misfortune has only occurred through my fault, considering I am what I am.' This was the occasion on which Vincent de Paul before abandoning the undertaking, called the general meeting of the Ladies of Charity which the painter's art has popularised. It was then that he made the appeal, which has ever since remained famous, and which was terminated by the splendid peroration that has always been regarded as a model of natural and spontaneous eloquence, gushing up, so to say, from the depths of his apostolic heart. 'And now, Ladies, compassion and charity led you to adopt these tiny creatures as your children ; you have been their mothers in the order of grace, since their mothers in the order of nature abandoned them. Consider now whether you too will abandon them. Cease to be their mothers and be their judges. Their life and death are in your hands. I am now about to take your votes ; the time has come to pronounce judgement, and to see if you are unwilling to have mercy on them. They will live if you continue to take a charitable care of them ; and on the contrary, they will infallibly perish and die if you abandon them ; experience will not allow you to think otherwise.' The Ladies, as Abelly, S. Vincent de Paul's biographer, tells us, ' were so touched that all unanimously resolved that the work must be carried on at no matter what cost.' But such an outburst of charity, after the first fervour had died down, was scarcely destined to last, and Mademoiselle Le Gras and her Daughters for many a long year had to resort to all manner of ingenious contrivances and countless privations to support the Foundling Hospital, the maintenance of which was left almost exclusively in their hands.

Whilst she was thus occupied in carrying on, with determination and amidst many and great anxieties, this work which has remained the most popular of all those due to her, ' Mademoiselle,' as she was always called by her own Daughters, did not neglect any of her other enterprises, and her field of action kept widening day by day. Quite a large number of ' charities ' were established in various places, especially at Fontainebleau, Chantilly, and Montreuil-sur-Mer, all of which had to be supplied with Sisters. Moreoever, a new ' charity ' which rapidly became a very important centre, was established in the parish of Saint-Sulpice. But it was especially during the troubled times of the civil war known as the Fronde that the charity of Louise de Marillac and her Daughters had to be multiplied in the midst of the general misery which ensued, not only in Paris, but in the Eastern and Northern Provinces, in Champagne and Picardy.

Ever by the side of Saint Vincent who multiplied himself, so to say, despite his advanced age and many infirmities, in his effort to improve the wretched lot of the poor, Louise de Marillac and her Daughters, during those years so terrible for the poorer classes, showed themselves fully worthy of their high calling. Both in Paris and the provinces they might have been seen spending themselves unsparingly in the service of the poor and wretched, nursing the sick, and also the plague-stricken, without the slightest hesitation and at the risk of their lives ; feeding the hungry and distributing the alms which Saint Vincent's ardent exhortations obtained from those who were still able to contribute ; in one word that sums up all, showing themselves to be true Daughters of Charity. In Paris, the Sisters distributed soup to the ' respectable poor ' and thus prevented them from dying of hunger. ' More than two thousand basins of soup are being made here for the respectable poor,' wrote Louise de Marillac, ' and the same holds true of other districts.' S. Vincent de Paul, on his side, wrote to one of his missionaries,[11] ' See how God is pleased that we should have a share in so many good undertakings. *The poor Daughters of Charity are doing more than we are* as far as the corporal assistance of the poor is concerned. They prepare and distribute soup every day, at Mademoiselle Le Gras' house, to thirteen hundred of the respectable poor, and in the Faubourg Saint-Denis, to eight hundred refugees.'

We regret we have no space here to describe at greater length all the works of charity undertaken by ' the good Sisters ' as the people had now begun to call them, and by their Mother, during these years of misery. We shall confine ourselves to quoting a passage from one of Vincent de Paul's letters which is more eloquent in its simplicity than much longer discourses could possibly be. He is replying to the Sisters of the ' charity ' at Valpuiseau, a village close to Étampes, who had asked that a Sister be sent from Paris to assist them as they were overburdened with work.[12] ' We would send a Sister to help you, if it were possible. But you know how difficult it is to travel just now ; moreover, sickness and poverty are so rife in Paris that Mademoiselle Le Gras has not enough Sisters to attend to the sick and the poor refugees. The Sisters are being asked for on all sides. Soup is being made for them in a large number of parishes ; our Sisters at Saint Paul's supply soup to more than eight thousand poor people every day, not to mention the sixty or eighty sick persons who are on their hands. Your Company has never worked so hard or so usefully than it is doing at the present moment. I trust that on this account God will bless it all the more. Your dear mother is quite well.'[12]

As a matter of fact, the Daughters of Mademoiselle Le Gras were now being asked for on all sides as the fame of their good deeds had been constantly spreading. They were even asked for in Poland, which, in those days when travelling was so difficult and so seldom undertaken, was regarded as being at the ends of the earth. The Queen of Poland, Marie Gonzaga, daughter of the Duke of Nevers, had been, before leaving France, one of the most zealous and active Ladies of Charity under Saint Vincent's direction ; when she became Queen she asked for Sisters of Charity, with whom she had already worked, and obtained Vincent de Paul's consent to send some Sisters to nurse the sick, to teach nursing, and to open schools for little girls.

S. Vincent de Paul, who saw a new field of action for his Daughters in Poland, had given his consent to the Queen's request readily enough. But Louise de Marillac found it harder to resign herself to sending those whom she had every right to call her children, six or seven hundred leagues off. However, duty called, and on September 7th, 1652, three Sisters chosen from amongst those of tried virtue set out for Poland, where they arrived on December 8, after a journey of three months. It was not without cause that ‘ the dear, good mother ’ of the Sisters of Charity who had been sent so far away amongst ‘ barbarians,’ as people would then have quite readily called the Poles, had seen their departure with fears and apprehensions. As a matter of fact, they were to encounter all manner of perils and trials : in the first place, a severe outbreak of plague was just then ravaging Warsaw and Poland ; next, the Swedes were conducting a fierce campaign against the King, John Casimir. They burned and pillaged wherever they went, and laid siege to the capital so that the Queen was compelled to fly before their furious hordes.

But this only offered an opportunity for the beloved Daughters of Louise de Marillac to show the extent of the devotedness they had learned in such an excellent school. Having nursed the plague-stricken, without thinking for a moment of the danger of contagion, they went to the battle-fields to tend the wounded, and showed such courage and self-sacrifice as to force the following involuntary cry of admiration from the lips of Saint Vincent himself, in the course of a conference in which he told the Sisters the news.[13]   'Now here is something that will undoubtedly cause you great joy. What!   Sisters are courageous enough to go to the armies!   Daughters of Charity, from the house in Paris, opposite Saint-Lazare, have gone to visit poor wounded soldiers, not only in France, but even in Poland. . . . Have you ever heard that anything like this was ever done before, that Daughters of Charity have gone to the armies for such a purpose?   As for me, I have never seen such a thing.   I do not know if there is any Company in existence which has accomplished the works that God has wrought through yours.'

It was, as a matter of fact, something quite new and one which astonished and surprised everybody, but we have since grown so accustomed to this spectacle, in the case of those very same Daughters of Louise de Marillac, that we almost forget to admire it, and we feel inclined to regard it as something quite natural.

And lastly, how can we pass over in silence the great part played by Mademoiselle Le Gras, during these same years, in the three great works of S. Vincent de Paul, whose faithful fellow-worker and welcome adviser she remained up to the end.   We are referring to the Hospital of the Holy Name of Jesus, the General Hospital, and the hospital known as 'The Little Houses.'   Not a single one of these three great works, with which Saint Vincent's name is so closely connected, was undertaken without the advice and co-operation of Louise de Marillac and her Daughters.

In 1653, Saint Vincent received a large sum of money from a generous citizen of Paris, whose name has remained unknown, to be employed on charitable works. It occurred to the saint that the money would be best spent in founding a hospital or 'home' for poor sick or aged artisans and workmen who could no longer earn a living. He consulted Mademoiselle Le Gras and she, after reflecting over the matter in prayer, decided that it was an excellent idea, and, together with her Daughters, undertook the charge of making the necessary preparations and of carrying on the work. 'Now,' she wrote in a note intended for Saint Vincent,[14] 'as this is an important work, and as it is essential to lay its foundations in such a way as to build it up in the best possible manner, and also to ensure its duration, it seemed to me that it would be advisable that the persons selected for it should be decent, honest folk, and most certainly not professional beggars.' After this, she went into all the details of how to organise the new establishment in such a clear-sighted way and with such practical suggestions as clearly reveal both the strength and prudence of her judgement.

S. Vincent de Paul, thus supported and encouraged by a woman who, whilst ever striving to efface herself, had such a remarkable intellect, which was indeed fully appreciated by the saint, now rented a house, in the month of October, in the Faubourg Saint-Laurent. The contract states : 'This house shall be employed as a place of retreat in which forty poor persons of both sexes shall be fed, clothed, and taught all those truths necessary for their salvation, whilst striving to lead them to live in the fear and love of God, and also to supply them with work so as to avoid mendicancy and idleness, the mother of all vices.' The Home was opened in October 1653 and called the Hospital of the Holy Name of Jesus. The success of the enterprise surpassed all expecta tions and especially those of its saintly foundress. Mademoiselle Le Gras took a quite particular interest in it up to the day of her death, and her Daughters devoted themselves to the work with their usual unselfish zeal. This actual hospital has survived, after passing through many a revolution, and is known at the present day as the Hospice for Incurables.

Next came the General Hospital, which struck the saint's contemporaries so forcibly, and on behalf of which Bossuet preached one of his greatest sermons. Louise de Marillac had a large share in this work, as she had in all the rest of S. Vincent de Paul's great undertakings. The Ladies of Charity, under Saint Vincent's direction, were anxious to make an attempt to open a large house of refuge into which would be admitted not merely poor people who had neither a home nor employment, but also the beg- gars who then infested the streets of Paris in crowds. The Ladies applied to Mademoiselle Le Gras for her opinion on the scheme, and asked if an appeal should be made to royal authority for its establish- ment. Although we cannot attempt to give a detailed account of this experiment, which was quite original in those days and which, as a matter of fact, was due to S. Vincent de Paul, we feel bound to give Louise de Marillac's reply to the Ladies, as it affords such a clear proof of the soundness and penetration of her intellect. 'If this enterprise,' she wrote,[15] 'is regarded as merely political (i.e. from the social point of view), then it seems to me it should be taken up by men. . . . If it is regarded as a work of charity, women could undertake it, just as they have undertaken other great and laborious exercises of charity of which God has shown His approval by granting them His blessings.'

Mademoiselle Le Gras, with a really remarkable clearsightedness combined with a sure and powerful judgement, thus laid down the conditions on which the work might be undertaken by the Ladies of Charity and at the same time remain a religious enterprise, that is to say, capable of inclusion within the ends and objects of the Association of the Ladies of Charity. 'It seems both impossible and undesirable that (the Ladies) should have sole responsibility,' she also declared, ' and it would be advisable if some devout men, who are either members of some organised society, or acting simply as private individuals, should be co-opted, both to give their advice, by expressing their views just as one of the Ladies might, and to take action in any law-suits or legal proceedings it may be necessary to embark on, in order to make these persons fulfil their obligations, on account of the diversity of their minds, characters and dispositions.

' Two or three things are to be desired : First, that the Ladies should submit their decision or any suggestions they may have to make to him whom

God has chosen to guide them ; secondly, that they should always act in the simple spirit in which they began, speaking out frankly what they think but without any passionate desire to have their own views carried out ; and thirdly, that the gentlemen who assist should not despise this manner of acting, although humanly speaking it might seem not to be reasonable, as it certainly is unusual : but experience has shown that God inspired it, and during the whole time the Ladies alone have been at work, the spirit of Christ has manifested itself amongst them by the graciousness, union and charity which has often led them to expose their lives for the love of God.'

S. Vincent de Paul was, no doubt, struck by the arguments brought forward which militated against the proposal, because he hesitated long before he embarked on this really formidable task.   Finally, urged by the Ladies of Charity, with the Duchesse d'Aiguillon as usual at their head, he yielded.   The Queen made a grant of the site of an old saltpetre factory which gave its name to the hospital, and at the present day it is still called ' La Salpêtrière.' Louise de Marillac sent some Sisters, for she could not afford very many, to set the new work going. As she had so clearly foreseen, the hospital soon became a *political* or, as we should say to-day, a social welfare institution, to which beggars and vagabonds were forcibly sent and compelled to re-main and work.   At the end of some years, the General Hospital had become simply a sort of prison placed at the disposal of the metropolitan police, under the ex-clusive control and management of the State.

In 1655, the members of the 'Central Office for the poor of Paris,' requested Mademoiselle Le Gras and her Daughters to take charge of the 'poor lunatics in the Asylum called The Little Houses.' In the ardour of her charitable zeal, she felt bound to accept this new mission, which was far more trying than any she had hitherto attempted. 'And as,' says her biographer, 'there are in this hospital, apart from the insane, a large number of old men who are maintained there by order of the Central Council, she also undertook to nurse them when they were ill.' This task of looking after poor lunatics was particularly difficult and terrifying, especially for women. The Brothers of S. John of God had only just established a house at Charenton for this object, and indeed, it is still in use for the same purpose at the present day. Moreoever, Mademoiselle Le Gras did not act without the advice and approbation of S. Vincent de Paul, under whose guidance she remained until her death. He gave her the greatest encouragement, and one day speaking at a conference to the Sisters, he cried out in moving tones :[16] 'Oh! my Daughters, my Daughters, how you have been favoured by God, and how deeply you are in His debt! Oh! my Daughters, how ungrateful you would be if you did not recognise this, and if you did not keep the rules of such a vocation which is so agreeable in the eyes of our Lord, and so profitable to your neighbour.' A few days later, he added :[17] 'Yes, my Daughters, it is God Himself who has willed to employ you to take care of those poor madmen. What a happiness that is for you all, and what a great favour for those who are being employed at it to have such a beautiful means of rendering this service to God and to our Lord, His Son! You know, my Daughters, that our Lord willed to experience in His own person every imaginable form of misery, because the Scripture tells us that He wished to be a scandal to the Jews and a folly to the Gentiles, so as to let you see how you can serve Him in all those poor afflicted people. And as it was His will to embrace this state in order to sanctify it like all others, it is essential for you to know that He is in those poor helpless creatures, deprived of the use of reason, just as He is in all the other sorts of poor people . . . and when you go and visit them you ought to rejoice that you are able to say to yourselves : " I am going to these poor creatures to honour in them the incarnate wisdom of a God who willed that He should be treated as a madman." '

One may well understand how language and emotion such as this excited the enthusiasm of Louise de Marillac and her Daughters. One of them very many years afterwards, at the process of canonisation of S. Vincent de Paul, said in reference to this conference : ' I remember that when the servant of God sent us to serve the poor lunatics in the asylum which had hitherto been badly managed, he gave us such a high idea of the favour God had granted us by entrusting us with this duty that we felt all on fire to devote ourselves to this work, notwithstanding the trials and difficulties that were to be met with in it.'

It was in this fashion that the work undertaken by Louise de Marillac, under the guidance of

Vincent de Paul, went on developing in various directions and ways with a rapidity that astonished all observers, and yet so peacefully, gently and quietly that no one seemed to notice that anything unusual or surprising had occurred. As for Louise de Marillac herself, she always remained the same, simple and devoted to all, and never for a moment thought that she was necessary. On the contrary, she was firmly convinced (with the humility of the saints which is so surprising to the world and in which it is so unwilling to believe, but which in reality is true and sincere for it proceeds from a supernatural, inner light) that she was the last and least of all God's creatures, whilst at the same time she preserved till the day of her death her fundamental originality and nobility of character.

If, for instance, the Mother of the Daughters of Charity remained up to the end the most tender and most vigilant of mothers in the order of grace and Christian charity, in the order of nature she was just as loving, and even retained that extreme sensitiveness which Saint Vincent had so often sought to calm. Her ' dear son Michel ' was always the object of her unceasing care, even in the midst of her hardest tasks. The young man was rather weak, undecided, lazy and without a spark of his mother's fire and activity. He long continued to cause her uneasiness, and his name keeps constantly cropping up in her letters. At last, in 1650, a marriage was arranged for him, and on January 18, 1650, as we have already mentioned, he married Gabrielle Le Clerc, daughter of Nicholas Le Clerc, Lord of the Manor of Chennevières, and Geneviève de La

N

[10] *Op. cit.*, Letter 266, p. 442.

[11] Baunard, *op. cit.*, p. 425.

[12] *Lettres de Saint Vincent de Paul*, Dumoulin ed. 1882, Vol. I, p. 435.

[13] *Conférences de Saint Vincent de Paul*, Conf. XLVII, p. 561.

[14] Louise de Marillac, *Écrits et Pensées*, No. 99, p. 265.

[15] *Écrits et Pensées de Louise de Marillac*, n. 112, p. 286.

[16] *Conférences de Saint Vincent de Paul*, Conf. LXII, p. 599.

[17] Baunard, *op. cit.*, p. 463.

[18] *Louise de Marillac*, Letter 275, p. 462.

CHAPTER VII

THE last years of the life of Louise de Marillac, whilst fully as active and fruitful in good works as those that had preceded them, are nevertheless characterised by a peace and tranquillity that impart to them a very special charm. They have the stillness and limpidity of a lovely day that is sinking to rest gilded by the beams of the setting sun. Her health, although gradually growing worse, was not allowed to interfere with her activity and zeal for all that is good, and the ever-increasing success of her work only served to render her more humble, more modest, more distrustful of herself and of her own lights. S. Vincent de Paul was always at her side and she was as respectful and submissive as in the past to him whom she continued to look upon to the end as ' her most honoured Father.' If the passing years had seen her growing more perfect in Christian detachment and advancing still further in the path of self-forgetfulness, which is its fruit, they had not diminished by an iota her charity and love for God and souls. Indeed, they perhaps increased them by enabling her to eliminate those traces of self-love and personal interest which are so tenacious and which spring up afresh even in the case of the best and even amidst the constant and courageous practice of the highest virtues and of their most difficult acts. Ever submissive to the voice of her spiritual guide, she devoted herself to the formation of her Daughters; she desired to make them more and more worthy of their vocation and better fitted to follow it, new as it was in form though not in spirit; she desired to assure in this way the most perfect execution of the works they had undertaken and also their gradual development.

This process of training 'good Daughters of Charity and true servants of the poor' was, in the declining years of Louise de Marillac, the one to which she devoted herself most earnestly and in which she best reveals herself. We shall see her then as she was during the last years of her life, and at the same time observe how these years were prolific in fruit both for herself and for others. But here, as on former occasions, an effort must be made if we desire to see her, as she took such pains to hide herself and, in a manner, to dissemble her influence and action. The sources on which we propose to rely, if we are to give even a partial portrait of Louise de Marillac in her last years, are those of her letters that have been preserved, letters of her Daughters in which they refer to their Superioress, the carefully preserved accounts in which the Sisters had given reminiscences of their 'dear Mother' and of Saint Vincent's conferences, in which he frequently refers to the examples given by 'Mademoiselle.' The limits of this sketch will not allow us to devote much space to the subject or to give a detailed analysis of her spirituality such as would perhaps be essential if it were to be a complete study, but even a few brief extracts may suffice to give at least some idea of it and also to show her in those last hours whose light was now beginning to shine uncertainly, if still graciously and truly.

In the first place, Louise de Marillac, who had always been first to set an example, endeavoured in particular to fashion those whom she was training to ' be good parish sisters,' simple and friendly, utterly devoted to their works of charity and their schools, yet never, for all that, forgetting their own sanctification and progress in the paths of the highest perfection. ' And indeed,' she remarked, ' I assure you I do not know any nuns who are more useful to the Church than are the Daughters of Charity on account of the services they render to their neighbour. Even the nuns in charge of the Hôtel-Dieu, who serve the sick, do not go outside the gates of the hospital in search of them. But you, you go in search of them as our Saviour was wont to do when He went from village to village healing the sick whom He met on the way. . . . Oh ! my Daughters, have you thought of that ? to do what God has done ! Should you not be perfect, and even in a way, angels in the flesh ? ' And in another place : ' If you wish to strive for perfection, my dear Sisters, you must die to yourselves. What a world of meaning is contained in those words ! Would that I could write them in my blood and leave them to you in letters of gold, my dearest friends in Jesus Christ.'[1]

Although she devoted herself particularly to the spiritual training of her Daughters in the private conferences which she held with them every week and which lasted for three-quarters of an hour, in familiar conversation, and during the hours of recreation, yet she never neglected any opportunity of instructing and forming them.   She gave the weekly conferences either on the Gospels, or on the mystery of the day, or on the devout life and the service of the poor, and ' although,' says her first biographer, ' she tried to speak to the Sisters simply, she could not prevent herself from explaining her meaning in a noble and elevated style, and she always spoke with an ardour which communicated itself to her hearers and which inspired them with the affection that filled her own heart.'   During the hours of recreation at which she assisted just as if she were a young novice, she was always gay and good-humoured, despite her poor health, the sadness of age, and the heavy cares that weighed her down.   Simplicity, cordiality, and gaiety were the distinguishing features of her conversation and she strove to communicate them to all around her.   In her letters she recommended Sisters who were grieving over their absence from her not to cry because she said weeping was as bad for the soul as it is for the body.   ' My dearest Sister,' she wrote to one of her Daughters whom she had sent to the provinces,[2] ' is it really true that you have been crying since you left Paris, and that if you could speak to that naughty Sister Louise who sent you away that you would tell her what you thought of her ?   If you have not done so, please let me know in writing because you are well aware how gladly I shall read your letter.'   And some time afterwards, writing to the same Sister, she says :[3] ' One of the chief things I recommend you, Sister Charlotte, is not to weep any longer or at least to cry as little as possible, because it is a far better thing to rejoice. Besides, what do we need seeing that wherever we are we have God with us.'

But the pretext of being glad and happy was not acceptable to Mademoiselle Le Gras if adduced as a motive for being absent from the community and moving about in the world without any necessity. ' The world sometimes reproaches us,' she said, ' for failing to respect it in certain circumstances ; but is very quickly edified when it sees that this results from the desire to practise virtue, whilst it very quickly notices those who allow themselves to be won by its applause.' Hence Daughters of Charity should never walk through the streets except when they have something definite to do and should derive their pleasure from their own society. ' All your conversations,' said Louise de Marillac to her Daughters, ' and all your consolations, if you can have any other than those of our Lord, should be found amongst yourselves.' But if the Sisters should avoid mixing with the world, whenever that is possible, yet they should always and towards all persons, practise *our dear virtue—friendliness*. ' The blessing of God,' she remarked, ' may be especially recognised in mutual forbearance and in cordiality, which are so necessary if Daughters of Charity are to be united and perfect. . . .'[4]

' If humility, simplicity and charity, which enable you to bear with one another, are firmly established amongst you, then your little Company will be

made up of as many saints as there are individuals
in it.' She herself put her teaching into practice
with an inexhaustible sweetness and patience towards those whom she had to guide and watch over.
It cannot, indeed, be said that she formed them
completely in the fullest sense of the word, because
she had neither the time nor the strength to do so,
on account of the delicate state of her health and the
multiplicity of her occupations. She showed the
greatest graciousness, tenderness, and charity to all
so that her teaching was singularly efficacious and
successful ; in this she was, indeed, the daughter of
S. Francis de Sales and of S. Vincent de Paul, her two
spiritual masters, and the pupil certainly did great
honour to both. Hence she always tried to help
Sisters to bear in a Christian manner whatever
misfortunes befell their families, and she did so
with a warmth and kindness that clearly show how
true charity does not dry up the heart's affections,
because, as the Scripture says, it establishes order
within it. 'My dear Sister,' she wrote on one
occasion when announcing the death of a relative,
'we should always await the dispensations of
Divine Providence with submission, whether it be
the death of one of our relations or our own, and
in such wise that the Divine Will may have no cause
for reproaching us for not having followed its
dispositions. I believe, my dear Sister, you do not
doubt that our Lord has willed to call a member of
your family home to Himself. . . . I beseech our
Lord to be your strength, your courage and your
consolation.' We shall also quote from a letter to
a Sister whose family were in want.[5] 'My dear

Daughter, your sister is in a pitiable condition considering the poverty in which she now is. But by God's grace she is bearing her misfortune in peace; pray for her and her three children. Your little brother has arrived in this city in the hope of being admitted into the Hospital for Incurables; we shall help him, if we possibly can. Your father has returned to Beauvais. Pray earnestly to God to grant him all the holy graces he stands in need of to bear his misfortunes bravely.'

It was in this way that ' dear, kind Mademoiselle ' showed an interest in her Daughters. She was not merely anxious to train them in their vocation, which duty, of course, held and was bound to hold, the first place in her eyes, but she also took a lively interest in their particular interests and affections, in all that concerned them, with a real mother's love and solicitude. Hence it is quite easy to imagine how they, who delighted to call themselves her children just as much as she did to call herself their mother, regarded her. So, too, the Sisters regarded Louise de Marillac's own family as their own, and, as we have said, the saint's little grand-daughter was looked on as one of themselves. ' The community,' wrote Louise to Sister Juliana,[6] ' will remember you when they are eating your lovely cakes; the *little sister* has not teeth enough yet to be able to eat any.'

' I thank you with all my heart,' she wrote on another occasion to Sister Louise,[7] ' for your affection for my son's little family. His hearing is now very much better, thank God; his wife is well and his little daughter, who was dangerously

ill, has now, by God's goodness, been restored to
him. They are in the country. I beg you to pray
to God for all their needs and especially for their
salvation.'

One may easily imagine how the Daughters of
Charity, trained with such care by a mother who was
really one in the best sense of the word, and instructed and guided by S. Vincent de Paul, were not
slow to win all hearts and to dissipate the prejudice
and astonishment which the new form of their
vocation may have excited in the beginning. People
grew quickly accustomed to see them in their
modest costume going through the streets of the
city as well as along the country roads, and they
were asked for in all quarters. The civil power,
which had at first manifested a certain mistrust in
their regard, quickly got rid of this impression,
and in the month of November 1657, the very
year in which, for the first time, the constitutions
of the Company were put into effect by the election
of ' officers ' entrusted with its government, the
royal approbation conferred a legal and definitive
existence on the new society. The King's Letters-
Patent approving of the Institute of the Sisters of
Charity were couched in the kindliest terms, and
rendered full justice to the Company.

It is stated in particular that the King,[8] ' wishing
to approve by his authority all good works and all
such establishments in his states as are carried on
for the glory of God ; and especially a society and
confraternity that has begun and progressed with
so much charity, hereby confirmed, approved and
authorised the aforesaid establishment for all parts

of France, taking it under his royal safeguard and protection, with power to possess and receive bequests, and donations, and to be immune from paying himself any tax or indemnity.' The approbation furthermore granted some very considerable privileges. The Royal Letters-Patent were registered in the Parliament and countersigned by Chancellor Séguier on December 16, 1658.

Papal approbation was not granted until ten years later, in 1668, after Louise de Marillac's death. But these delays, typical of the prudent conduct of the Court of Rome, implied no mistrust on its part, and were simply in conformity with canonical procedure. Pope Innocent X, indeed, had never ceased to show a special interest and friendliness towards the new undertaking, and in 1647 had even bestowed his apostolic blessing, by a special brief, on Mademoiselle Le Gras and her Daughters. This blessing was applicable at the hour of death, and it was a favour, as we shall soon see, to which she attached the greatest value and for which she was abundantly grateful.

The King's Letters-Patent, which thus gave a legal existence to Louise de Marillac's ' little Company ' and greatly facilitated its development, did in point of fact simply set a seal on results that had already been obtained, for during the last years of its foundress, the work, of its own momentum and without any positive contribution on her part, rapidly extended. From all directions calls were coming for ' the good Daughters of Charity ' for hospitals, schools, parochial ' houses of Charity,' or ' of Mercy,' and Louise de Marillac was unable to meet these demands ; often indeed she could only reply with a refusal, as the number of Sisters was still very small.

In 1654, she had to send some Sisters to Sedan to nurse the wounded, at the express and personal request of Queen Anne of Austria who had seen them at work and thoroughly appreciated their worth. It was impossible to refuse such a request, however nervous the Superiors may have felt about sending them on such a mission.[9] ' You have been selected then,' said Saint Vincent in one of his conferences, ' to go and comfort the poor men who have been wounded in the King's service, and on that account I think it would be well to consider the motives you have for giving yourselves to God to carry out this duty well.

' And the first is that you have been chosen—and by whom, Sisters ? Oh ! by God Himself who has thus turned to you. Although there are plenty of young women in Sedan and the neighbourhood, still they have not been thought of, so it is not to the young women of Sedan God has turned, but to the Daughters of Charity from amongst all those of France, and to you, my Daughters, from amongst all your Sisters. It is the Queen who has asked for you. What ! Sisters ! Who are we that the greatest Queen in the world should think about us ? We are only poor, wretched creatures, not to say beggars. Yes, my Daughters, and you and I, therefore, have great reason to humble ourselves.' Two years later, in 1656, it became necessary to send Sisters to Arras, where, as at Sedan, they were summoned to nurse wounded soldiers, and where,

in matter of fact, they appeared for the first time
outside the walls of a hospital. They nursed the
wounded in ambulances and on the battlefield in
the modest costume of a Sister of Charity which has
since been so often seen bearing help and consolation everywhere in its train. ' The Daughters of
Charity went, despite the novelty of the work and
its dangers, with their usual simplicity and courage,
praying to God, as Louise de Marillac had recommended them, for the King's army and for the conversion of the enemy, because as for our dear France,
she added, we are already under too many obligations to her to recommend her to you.'[10]

In 1658, shortly after the Battle of the Dunes, the
Queen called the Sisters to Calais to nurse the
soldiers who had been attacked by an epidemic
disease. Saint Vincent, much moved by this new
testimony to his Daughters' worth, could not refrain
from saying to them before their departure :[11]
' What a motive for humbling yourselves, Sisters,
seeing how God wishes to make use of you for such
great things ! Oh ! Saviour ! Men go to war to
slay their fellow-men and you, my Daughters, you
go to repair the ills they cause. Oh ! what a blessing
from God ! Men slay the body and often enough
the soul ; you are going to restore life to both, or
at least to help to preserve it in those who remain,
striving by your good example as well as by your
instructions to make them see that they ought to
conform themselves to the Will of God in their
state in life. . . . I know that, by God's grace,
there are many of you who are quite ready to go
when called on. Yes, I know there are some who

will ask nothing else than just simply where they are
to go, and who will say : God is my Father, let
Him place me on the right hand, that is at my ease,
or on the left hand, which signifies the Cross ; it
does not matter ; He will, I hope, strengthen me.
Now, that is how a good Daughter of Charity acts,
who has no other will than the will of God. Oh !
happy servitude ! . . . So, then, be you all prepared
to do what God wishes you to do, and seek for
nothing, neither to be in this house, nor in this
prison, nor in such and such a country place, and
neither have any fear to go wherever you may be
sent. Consider that wherever you may go God will
take care of you. Believe that firmly and never lose
the confidence you should have in Providence, and
even if you should happen to be in the midst of
armies, never fear that any ill will befall you. Has
any ill befallen those who are already there ? Has
any Sister received an injury, or has any one died ?
And even if she did lose her life, oh ! that would be
well for her for she would have died as a true
soldier of Christ, and have gone straight to God
laden with merits.'

As if to justify S. Vincent de Paul's words, the
Sisters who had gone to Calais were attacked by the
contagious disease whose victims they had been
sent to nurse, and one of the Sisters died of it. When
news of this reached Paris, twenty others volun-
teered to replace her with such ardour and self-
forgetfulness as to afford the deepest consolation to
Louise de Marillac. Amongst them was Sister
Henrietta who had already begged to go and nurse
the wounded at Sedan, in the height of the Fronde,

' like,' as Mademoiselle Le Gras expressed it, ' a
soldier who hears the trumpet sound for action.'
And S. Vincent de Paul was so touched by the spirit
of self-sacrifice in his ' Daughters ' that he referred
to it in the following terms, when speaking to his
confrères : ' Observe, Gentlemen and my Brethren,
the courage of these girls in offering themselves as
victims for the love of Jesus Christ and of their
neighbour. Is it not wonderful ? As for me, I do
not know what to say about it except that these girls
will be our judges at the Day of Judgement. Yes,
they will be our judges if we are not prepared like
them to risk our lives for God.'[12]

The reputation of the Daughters of Charity had
travelled beyond the borders of France, and re-
quests had been made that they should go to other
countries. In 1652, as we have said, the famous
and lively Marie de Gonzaga, Queen of Poland,
had summoned them to her side, and another group
of Sisters had to be sent to Warsaw in 1657. ' Yes,
my Daughters,' said Saint Vincent to them, [13] ' your
name is spreading in all directions ; it is even known
as far away as Madagascar where they are anxious
to have you. Our priests who are in that distant
land have written to us that it would be desirable for
you to have an establishment there so that the souls
of the poor negroes might be more easily won for
God. Oh ! my Daughters, it is God who is blessing
your Company, and He will always bless it more and
more if you are faithful.' Louise de Marillac, for
her part, wrote to one of the Sisters :[14] ' Oh ! what
a blessed journey it would be to go to Madagascar !
I think it is not more than from a thousand to a

thousand two hundred leagues away.' And, in January 1658, she writes again :[15] 'A great number of our Sisters are most anxious that the expedition to Madagascar will not sail without them.' Their ardour showed no sign of diminishing as the years went by, and the prophecy with which S. Vincent de Paul ended one of his conferences was realised to the letter, as we may see to-day. 'The day will come, Sisters,' he said to them, 'when God will send you to Africa and the Indies.'

It was in this fashion, faithful to her work unto the last, devoting herself entirely to the training of her Daughters, labouring unceasingly and silently, within herself, to use the seventeenth-century phrase, which conveys the idea of working out her own perfection and of acquiring complete detachment from self, that Louise de Marillac saw death approaching, and his arrival was not to be delayed for long. Her days were in truth numbered, and everything pointed to the fact that the supreme moment was not far distant. Her health, long deplorable, was continually growing worse, and she had grown so weak and completely exhausted that she seemed to live as if by a miracle. Moreover, she saw her faithful friends and collaborators from the beginning passing away one after another. The well-beloved 'Monsieur Vincent,' who had now become for all Sisters of Charity 'Our most honoured Father' was now eighty years old, growing more and more infirm, and able to visit 'his dear Daughter' very rarely. Soon he was not able to leave the precincts of Saint-Lazare.

Louise de Marillac bore all these privations uncom-

o

plainingly ; her only fear now was lest she might feel them too keenly and she unceasingly longed for the day when, her trials all over, she might hope to enjoy eternal happiness.   However, her wishes and desires were without a shade of self-seeking and were marked by a touching simplicity.   ' When I was recovering from my last severe illness,' she wrote in a memorandum still extant,[16] ' I asked M. Vincent, our most honoured Superior and Founder, what should be the state of mind in which I should renew my resolutions to begin life anew.   His Charity told me, amongst other pieces of advice conformable to the Will of God, that I should deny myself what pleases self and practise renunciation.'   Hence, as soon as she felt sufficiently well, she set to work once more and laboured at the training of the Sisters, but in complete conformity with the Will of God.   ' Allow me, my most honoured Father,' she wrote to Saint Vincent,[17] ' to tell you that my powerlessness to do any good whatever prevents me from having anything acceptable to offer to our Lord, except the poor renewal of my service, and the deprivation of the only consolation His loving-kindness had given me for the last thirty-five years. I accept it for His love and in the manner that Providence has ordained.'   She is referring to S. Vincent de Paul's inability to visit her any longer. In another letters she says :[18] ' It seems to me that our Lord has now placed me in a state in which I can henceforth bear all things fairly patiently, and I am bound to do so since I have the honour to be, my most honoured Father, your most humble, obedient and obliged daughter and servant.'

On February 4, 1660, Louise de Marillac took to her bed, from which she was nevermore to rise. She was suffering from acute inflammation of her shoulder which had been severely crushed by a fall many years previously and which had never quite healed. To this was added a violent attack of fever which soon put her in danger of death and which was in no way diminished by blood-letting, the remedy then in vogue. The inflammation soon became so violent and the danger of death so imminent that it seemed to be necessary for her to receive the Last Sacraments immediately. She was suffering acutely but with the patience and calm she had always shown in like circumstances. Such dispositions were indeed great graces from God, yet they did not diminish either the pain of her sufferings or remove the difficulty of enduring them. ' It is necessary in truth,' she said, ' that pain abides where sin has abounded. God is acting as a Judge, and whilst executing justice He grants mercy.'

She received Holy Viaticum and Extreme Unction; her sufferings were at this stage so acute that she could not help crying aloud in the presence of her children who were grouped around her—(that is to say, Michel Le Gras, and his wife and daughter, then nine years old)—' Oh ! my children, how one must suffer before death ! ' After she had received the last Sacraments, she turned towards them and said with a solemnity befitting the occasion : ' My dear children, I pray God, the Father, the Son, and the Holy Ghost, by the power He has given fathers and mothers to bless their children, to bless you, to detach you from all earthly things, and to unite you to Himself.' . . . ' Then turning her eyes towards the Daughters of Charity,' as the account of the last moments of Louise de Marillac tells us, ' she also gave them her blessing and recommended them to love their vocation, and to be faithful in their service of the poor.'[19]

S. Vincent de Paul and all the Sisters were deeply grieved. ' She has fallen so ill,' wrote the saint,[20] ' that we do not dare hope for her recovery and this greatly afflicts us ; our sorrow is heightened by the fact that Father Portail is also gravely ill. They both received the Holy Viaticum on the same day.' S. Vincent's friend and untiring collaborator, Fr. Portail, died, in fact, shortly afterwards. But Mademoiselle Le Gras lasted longer than had been anticipated, as God no doubt wished to complete the work of her sanctification. ' When Fr. Portail was dying,' said Saint Vincent,[21] ' Mademoiselle Le Gras was also at the point of death and we thought she would go before him. But she is still alive and is recovering, thanks be to God, who has not been pleased to load us with a double burden of affliction.'

The poor invalid lingered on for another three weeks, and her community even believed for a moment that she had been preserved to them by prayer, but it was only a respite or rather an occasion for an increase of merit and purification, for she never ceased to suffer both from her illness and from the remedies employed to counteract it, such as the letting of blood and incisions. She bore it all without complaint or murmur, prepared for death if God should call her, and ready to live on if the Divine Will and the welfare of her Daughters demanded, because the good of her Daughters was, during her last hours, her chief preoccupation. ' As I wished to know,' one of them tell us,[22] ' what she would ask from God for me and for all our Sisters, she told me she would ask for the grace that we might live like true Daughters of Charity in great union and cordiality, and that those who would do so would have a great reward. But as for those who would not . . . she paused and did not finish her remark.' On March 9, her illness grew worse and gangrene set in in her injured arm. She asked for the Holy Viaticum once more, and on the 14th of the month, she had the happiness she so ardently longed for. ' She edified and moved the bystanders to tears,' says her first biographer,[23] ' by the sentiments of respect and love she manifested in this holy action, and, her pastor exhorting her to give her blessing once more to her Daughters, she uttered the following words, which she left them as her last will and testament : ' My dear Sisters, I continue to ask God to bless you and I beseech Him to grant you the grace to persevere in your vocation so that you may serve Him in the way He expects of you. Be very diligent in the service of the poor, and above all, be careful to live together in great union and cordiality, loving one another in imitation of the union and life of our Lord. And pray earnestly to the Blessed Virgin that she may be your only Mother.' She added that she died ' with the loftiest idea of their vocation and that if she were to live to be a hundred she would always recommend them the same thing.'

' Her illness could not interrupt the exercise of her charity ; she always kept herself informed as to whether the poor of the parish were being looked after and who were then being fed in her house, and she gave orders as if she were in perfect health.

' One of the greatest trials she ever experienced was that which God sent her in this illness by depriving her of Saint Vincent's assistance. He was then so infirm as to be unable to pay her a single visit. But as she saw he was powerless to render her, in the hour of death, that office of charity which she had so ardently desired, she sent to ask at least for some words of consolation written by himself ; but her virtue was put to a final test for this wise director did not think it expedient to grant her this favour and merely sent her one of the priests of his congregation with orders to tell her from him that she was going before him and that he hoped to see her soon in Heaven. Although nothing was more calculated to affect her than this privation, she received it with extraordinary tranquillity and moderation and remained inseparably attached and united to the good pleasure of God.'[24]

At length, on March 15, 1660, Louise de Marillac, surrounded by her Daughters and sustained by her ever ardent faith, peacefully fell asleep in the Lord. ' On the morning of her last day on earth, the Sisters who had charge of the children came to see her. When she saw them on their knees close to her bed, she said : " Rise up, Sisters," and as she found it very difficult to speak, she merely added : " Good-bye, Sisters, be very careful in the service of the poor." About eleven o'clock in the morning, she had the curtain of her bed raised, as she had promised, to let her Daughters know that her hour was approaching, and she entered on her death-agony. It lasted for about half an hour, during which her eyes were constantly raised to Heaven. The Duchess de Ventadour, who had spent part of the night by her bed, did not leave her until after she had emitted her last breath, and she held the lighted candle in her old friend's hand. The prayers for a departing soul were recited and she heard them quite clearly, making the responses to them interiorly by the sentiments of her heart.'[25]

' A priest of the Congregation of the Mission then said to her : " Would you not like to give your blessing again to your Daughters ? " They were kneeling around her. She said with great difficulty to those who were at the foot of her bed : " I should like to have all our Sisters here, but you can tell the others." She then added : " I beseech our Lord to give you the grace to live like true Daughters of Charity in peace and union."

' After that, the priest asked her if she wished to receive the Apostolic Benediction at the hour of death which she had obtained from Pope Innocent X for herself and her Daughters, by a Brief dated September 24, 1647. She replied : " It is not yet time." Shortly afterwards, she said : " Soon, soon." They asked her if it were the Apostolic Benediction she required. She said in a very low voice : " Yes." She struck her breast three times and received it with the greatest devotion. She then had the curtains of her bed lowered and after half an hour passed away so quietly that although all were looking at her attentively, they could not believe she had expired.

'Thus died Louise de Marillac on Sunday in Passion Week, on March 15, 1660, between eleven o'clock and midday, aged seventy years, seven months and four days. The parish priest of S. Lawrence, who was present at the end of her agony, said after she had expired : "Farewell, oh, blessed soul !" When he was about to leave he said that she had preserved her baptismal innocence all her life. Her body was laid out on a bed for a day and a half to satisfy the wishes of several ladies who desired to have the consolation of seeing her once more after her death, and to render her the last tributes of their love and veneration.'

As the contemporary record, from which we have taken most of the above details, has told us, the body of Louise de Marillac was exposed for a day and a half to afford an opportunity to her Daughters and the devout women to whom she had been a model, and even more, the tenderest of mothers, of seeing her for the last time calm and serene in death. On the following Wednesday, the remains of Mademoiselle Le Gras were buried in the Church of S. Lawrence, 'in the chapel of the Visitation of the Blessed Virgin in which she was wont to pray, and although she had meant to be buried in a cemetery close to S. Lawrence's, M. Vincent nevertheless thought it fitting to fall in with the pastor's request and allow him to have this precious treasure for his parish, so that the mother's body should not be separated from the remains of her Daughters who had gone before her. . . .